T0146905

MANAGERS—GETTING THE >>> RIGHT START

BOB EPLEY

MANAGERS—GETTING THE RIGHT START

iUniverse books may be ordered through booksellers or by contacting:

iUniverse
1663 Liberty Drive
Bloomington, IN 47403
www.iuniverse.com
1-800-Authors (1-800-288-4677)

ISBN: 978-1-5320-2698-0 (sc)
ISBN: 978-1-5320-2699-7 (e)

Library of Congress Control Number: 2017911875

Print information available on the last page.

iUniverse rev. date: 09/14/2017

CONTENTS

INTRODUCTION

Throughout my career I encountered a wide variety of management approaches. I took note of the stylistic distinctions and the relative effectiveness attached to each one. Ultimately I reached the conclusion that most of the managers I worked for and with did not really have a plan to engineer improvements in their organizations. The common approach was to work harder and put in more hours. This led to mixed results. Sometimes there were short-term improvements, but most often those gains dissipated over time because they were not accompanied by systemic improvements. When working harder didn't succeed, the next step seemed to be updating our processing systems or hiring outside consultants to analyze our problems.

As I moved into positions that offered more responsibility, opportunities to work with consultants from private firms increased. In most instances these firms were hired to help us execute large, high-priority projects. My overall observation was that the consultants were uniformly bright and knowledgeable, and they always had multiple suggestions for tackling our issues. But the solutions were almost all tool based, meaning the solutions were better, more sophisticated support tools and IT systems that addressed specific problems and did not help with overall operations. We used charts and graphs to describe project development and progress, but it was extremely rare to find an area where consultants or in-house analysts consciously examined our basic approach to managing the business as a whole. This always seemed to be treated as a given and was too basic to analyze. I think it was, and still is, a mistake.

Much of the material in this book grew from my early observations and later attempts to execute various management approaches in a range of settings. Much of my learning about management activities was gained through trial and error. Fortunately, I was given sufficient latitude to try various approaches, as long as I produced acceptable outputs. And I learned.

I believe some of the lessons I picked up along the way can be beneficial to newly appointed managers or to managers who find themselves in an awkward setting where they are having trouble moving forward. Addressing this is the premise of this book, which offers guidance for people who are moving into a new management position, especially those who have not previously held management jobs.

Management of a business operation is complicated. The work of a manager is fundamentally different from that of production workers and technicians. As a new manager, or one recently promoted to a higher position, you are about to embark on a remarkable journey. Some parts of the road will be rocky and challenging; others will be smooth. A lot of factors will come into play. Usually, the environment will be dynamic, and you, the newly appointed manager, will have to adapt quickly to change. Unfortunately, I don't think the complex nature of such a position is always appreciated by new incumbents.

My experience is that often the best technician in an operation is picked to assume the office manager's role when it is vacated. Those "best technicians" are intelligent and confident, and they feel sure they can perform as well as their predecessor. But just as often, these new appointees do not have management training or experience, and the difficulties associated with their new position are greater than they expected. So their new job proves to be more challenging than they anticipated.

Managers—Getting the Right Start is not intended to be comprehensive or self-sufficient. Rather, it's intended to be an introductory aid, a primer that will help get you started in a management role and give you enough tools so that you can build a successful foundation. The guidance will help you avoid missteps and quickly get to the point of being effective and productive. From that point you can expand your foundation, move on to tackle other, more complex challenges, more broadly develop your skills, and incorporate more sophisticated approaches.

To do this I will discuss subjects that will be important for an incoming manager:

- how you understand the concepts of mission, vision, and organizational strategy
- how you discuss where you fit in to your organization's execution of those important fundamentals
- how you build and organize your systems and procedures
- how you develop your people
- how you relate to those outside your own work group
- how you monitor your progress

Within these basic subject areas are subtopics, like communications or business relationships, that span more than one area. In those instances I discuss the subtopics in more than one place so the broader topical areas are covered inclusively. This facilitates the flow of discussion.

Implementing these basic management steps will facilitate development of strong, positive relationships with your boss, your colleagues on other staffs you work with (sister staffs), and your employees. The book will also guide you to take the necessary actions to maintain your new business relationships. Finally, this book will help you build effective oversight systems so that you can stay on course and build a successful operation.

CHAPTER 1
YOU AS A MANAGER

Managers—Getting the Right Start offers guidance on getting a strong start in a new management position and how to construct a solid foundation.

I worked for the federal government for more than thirty years and have worked with private companies for several more years since I "retired." When I started my career, I took an entry-level position and had little direct contact with managers. They were in offices on a different floor. Because they represented an unknown to me, my mind conjured up various images, based on my limited experiences, including TV shows of the 1950s and '60s. I'm sure others have conjured up hundreds of composites for the stereotypical manager: he is "the big boss"; he is male; he smokes cigars; he is overweight and slightly disheveled; he talks roughly and barks orders from his office desk to some unknown and unseen minions, who rush to carry out his demands.

On the other end of the stereotype spectrum is the manager as a meticulously neat man or woman in a dark blue suit, white shirt, and appropriately contrasting necktie or scarf; hair is perfectly styled; briefcase is new and made of rich, soft leather; and he or she is freshly graduated from a reputable MBA program.

As my career advanced, I worked directly with managers and occupied some management slots myself. Those experiences exposed me to many different images of a manager. My perception of what this should be evolved over time, as my experiences grew. I came to understand they come in all sizes and shapes and have innumerable combinations of strengths and weaknesses. I never met the perfect prototype, but I did encounter several good, successful managers.

My early, extreme manager images clearly reflected my own ignorance and biases. We would not want to use these rough, simplistic images as the prototype of today, although I hope we can learn from them. The cigar-smoking barker was decisive and got things done. Didn't generate a lot of teamwork, though. The crisp and clean MBA images probably reflect a feeling that education and a professional appearance were important attributes, and they are—they just don't guarantee success. The description of an immaculate person in the perfectly pressed suit leaves one with the thought that he or she never rolled up their sleeves and investigated a problem.

So even though both early composites probably contain some positive characteristics, we can surely build a better prototype.

I want to describe a man or woman not too different from you and me as the prototype. My prototype has pretty good analytical skills, common sense, and sound communications and people skills; this individual has an ego but one that is properly sized and under control. He or she understands the importance of a professional appearance but is not obsessed with it. Our manager has the ability to see the issues that are important, and he or she can effectively focus on them.

What does a person do when managing? In his book *The Practice of Management*, Peter F. Drucker puts it this way:

> Despite its crucial importance, its high visibility, and its spectacular rise, management is the least known and the least understood of our basic institutions. Even the people in a business often do not know what their management does and what it is supposed to be doing, how it acts and why, whether it does a good

job or not. Indeed, the typical picture of what goes on in the "front office" or on "the fourteenth floor" in the minds of otherwise sane, well-informed, and intelligent employees (including, often, people themselves in responsible managerial and specialist positions) bears striking resemblance to the medieval geographer's picture of Africa as the stomping ground of the one-eyed ogre, the two-headed pygmy, the immortal phoenix, and the elusive unicorn. What then is management: What does it do?

There are two popular answers. One is that management is the people at the top—the term "management" being little more than euphemism for "the boss." The other one defines a manager as someone who directs the work of others and who, as a slogan puts, "does his work by getting other people to do theirs."

The first definition of management is therefore that it is an economic organ, indeed the specifically economic organ of an industrial society. Every act, every decision, every deliberation of management has as its first dimension an economic dimension. (1954, 6)

Edward Lawler (1986) put it this way:

Overall, managers in high-involvement organizations need a particular set of leadership skills that will allow them to do four critical things for the organization:

1. build trust and openness;
2. provide a vision and communicate it;
3. move decisions to the proper location; and
4. empower others.

The thoughts above offer a number of descriptors for management, including one who directs, is in charge of things, controls, and guides. These are all active terms, and they imply that the manager ensures that things move in the right direction.

Using this as a base, I will use "management" to mean the business (or the act) of guiding an organization's activities so that the proper outputs and outcomes are produced at an acceptable pace, ensuring that the organization functions effectively enough to sustain itself.

I will describe the types of actions, communications, systems, and procedures that managers should design and deploy to get the right results. There is no single, clear combination of ingredients that mix into successful management. Rather, several combinations of approaches and tools can be successful. But there are minimum requirements, and I will discuss those.

In some ways the manager is like the conductor of an orchestra. Orchestra members bring certain skills. They each know what music they are supposed to play. The conductor blends the individual musicians together. He or she tells them when to start, when to stop, when to play boldly or softly. He or she brings synergy to the individual pieces. He or she ensures the musicians pace themselves so they all finish at the same time. The conductor doesn't play the music; he or she ensures that the music gets played correctly and beautifully—period.

Similarly with the manager, he or she doesn't *do* the individual components of the work; he or she makes sure they *get done*.

Drucker describes it this way:

> [M]anagement has to *manage*. And managing is not just passive, adaptive behavior; it means taking action to make the desired results come to pass ... But it is also clear that the "resources" capable of enlargement can only be human resources. All other resources stand under the laws of mechanics. They can be better utilized or worse utilized, but they can never have an

output greater than the sum of the inputs ... The final function of management is to manage workers and work ... This implies organization of the work so as to make it most suitable for human beings, and organization of people so as to make them work most productively and effectively. (1954, 11–14)

Lawler says, "Yes, walking around is important, but it is not enough. Leaders must be able to engage in meaningful conversation and quickly develop a sense of the way things are going" (Lawler 1986).

Knowing what a manager does is important. It is also valuable to understand the competencies that facilitate good management. Because it involves dealing with fluid environments, handling unexpected occurrences, and steering through them to keep the organization moving in the right direction, possession of certain traits or competencies facilitates the process. I think most people would agree that a good manager should have sound judgment, resourcefulness, and good communications skills.

But there are certainly numerous other skills that can improve the effectiveness of a manager. Absorbing these traits and refining them over time through practice and repetition will help you to grow as a leader. Hopefully, in the ensuing pages it will become evident how various traits meld into the day-to-day activities that managers can expect to face.

It can be worthwhile to do periodic self-assessments of your skills and competencies. You need to know what your strengths and weaknesses are. You should actively work to develop the areas where you are less comfortable, and check your progress.

It is also appropriate to seek the advice of your supervisor when reviewing these competencies. He or she may have a different view of your strengths and weaknesses. That alone would be beneficial to know. Since a large measure of your success is the degree to which you satisfy your supervisor's expectations, you need to be sure you stay in touch with his or her assessments. If there are areas where your self-assessment varies from your supervisor's views, you may have a strong incentive to reconcile those differences.

Finally, to make sure your self-image regarding management style and approaches is consistent with the way your organization as a whole views you, ask colleagues to evaluate your use of the various competencies and effectiveness with them. By inviting the broadest possible feedback, you increase likelihood that you get the right information to continue your management growth.

Through all of this attention to management competencies, it's important to remember what the workers of the organization need. Warren Bennis said it well in his book *On Becoming a Leader* (1985): "The most important point I can make about leadership in light of the seismic changes taking place in our global economy is that followers need from their leaders three basic qualities: they want direction; they want trust; and they want hope."

In the area of self-analysis and performance assessments, be proactive. It is too common that managers shy away from performance reviews of their employees. It is even more common that all employees—not just managers—avoid real self-assessments. You can't improve unless you know where your developmental gaps are, and you won't know where the gaps are unless you gather data and review it.

There will be many times where the terms manager and leader seem interchangeable. This is because the literature tends to overuse the term "leader" and use it when "manager" is really the proper term. It seems the common belief is that leadership is a natural progression from management roles. I disagree with this. Management is about getting things done. The manager instructs, guides, and oversees the activities of her or his unit. A good manager exhibits many characteristics that are generally attached to leadership, such as honesty, passion, integrity, boldness, and creativity. Aspiring to be a good manager should be a positive and worthwhile pursuit.

Leadership is different. It's much bigger. Leadership is represented in a person by the combination of beliefs, compassion, and actions that causes people to trust in, believe in, and follow a person. Someone becomes a leader when others willingly follow.

Because leadership is bestowed upon a person by those who would follow him or her, it is a special attribute. But it's also not automatically or necessarily a good thing. A person with leadership qualities can lead people in bad directions. Does the name Hitler ring any bells? Keep this in mind as you assess your own leadership skills and style.

Bennis puts its well by saying, "To an extent, leadership is like beauty: it's hard to define, but you know it when you see it" (1985, 1).

He explains further by saying

> Leaders come in every size, shape, and disposition— short, tall, neat, sloppy, young, old, male, and female. Nevertheless, they all seem to share some if not all of the following ingredients:
>
> - The first basic ingredient of leadership is a guiding vision ...
> - The second basic ingredient of leadership is *passion*—the underlying passion for the promises of life, combined with a particular passion for a vocation, a profession, a course of action ...
> - The next basic ingredient of leadership is *integrity*. I think there are three essential parts of integrity: self-knowledge, candor, and maturity ...
> - Integrity is the basis of *trust*, which is not as much an ingredient of leadership as it is a product. It is the one quality that cannot be acquired, but must be earned ...
> - Two more basic ingredients of leadership are curiosity and daring. The leader wonders about everything, wants to learn as much as he can, is willing to take risks, experiment, try new things. He does not worry about failure but embraces errors, knowing he will learn from them. (1985, 39–41)

Managers should strive to be leaders. They need to understand that work will be done far more effectively if people take their instructions and requests willingly. If the workers do only as requested because they must, their performance will be average at best.

As you read these somewhat interchangeable terms, you decide which better applies.

Among the most basic things a manager must understand is the part he or she should play in the new organization and how he or she fits in.

The role of a manager relates to the defined area of his or her work, the scope of his or her responsibility, and any guidance the organization provides about how to execute the managerial functions. For example, a new manager may be given responsibility for taking in new business orders for the entire United States; or he or she may share that responsibility geographically with two other peers. In either case, that manager will have expectations for interactions with staffs that will receive the business orders from the manager's staff. If a manager shares jurisdiction with two peers, that individual must devote considerable energy coordinating with those peers. If the manager is responsible for monitoring the entire geographic United States, though, he or she may set up communications with other staffs a little differently. There would be no need to coordinate policies and procedures with a sister staff.

A manager with responsibility for an entire work process, from inception through completion, may have a fair amount of latitude in adjusting the processes. A manager who handles a narrow part of a larger, complicated process will be restricted by the narrow scope of responsibility. He or she will probably spend a lot of energy refining individual steps to improve efficiency.

The type of output a team produces also defines the manager's role. The manager of a mailroom operation will have very specific and recurring time schedules; his or her oversight role will be focused on the short term. The manager of a system development team may take a significantly different approach to his or her role and have much longer timelines between milestones.

There are many styles of management. Most can work satisfactorily under proper circumstances. Many will facilitate excellent results under the right conditions. I will not try to summarize the full range of styles; that is beyond the scope of this book. Rather, I have drawn on my own experience, and the guidance in this book reflects my observations.

In today's world, more and more people are earning advanced degrees, and learning is as close as a touch of your notebook or laptop. This environment lends itself to a more collaborative and less directive style of management than may have been common years ago. As our workforce has grown and become more sophisticated, the authoritative style that was common in previous generations has become less acceptable.

What follows in this book assumes a collaborative or participative management approach. Participative management is not a new or radical concept, and it still fits in our modern business environment. It has been described in many different ways, and I will use the term as follows: it is a type of management in which employees at all levels are encouraged to contribute ideas toward identifying and setting organizational goals; problem solving; and contributing to other decisions that may directly affect them.

Our employees are getting more educated every day. They are intelligent and have good ideas about how to get things done effectively. It is in a manager's best interest to listen to their ideas, indeed to encourage employees to voice their thoughts. Also, these highly educated employees are decreasingly likely to be satisfied with jobs that simply direct them to follow repetitive steps and not consider potential process improvements.

Excellent managers need to be able to adapt their styles to specific situations, though. There will be times when quick, decisive action is needed. At other times you may need to wait for more deliberation or let go of the controls to get the right solutions.

Appropriately adapting your style and approach to the unique circumstances in order to fit the development level of the followers you are trying to influence—sometimes called situational leadership—is an important skill. Those are the things that can make a management role satisfying. You get to adapt to the specific situation in front of you.

Mike Krzyzewski, coach of the Duke University basketball team, put it well in his book, *Leading with the Heart*:

> In general, my style is to be flexible and versatile. In other words, I think there's a time to get in someone's face and there's a time when you just put it on the line without yelling. There's also a time when you pat on the back. And there's a time when you hug.
>
> The only way to know when to do what is to look at each situation differently. Each moment requires its own maneuver.
>
> In that same vein, it's also important to remember that every person is different and has to be motivated differently. One player might respond to a pat on the rear, another might need to be kicked in the rear. And still another might need no attention at all. Some people respond when you challenge them, others when you encourage them. Some people respond when criticized. And some go into a shell with even the slightest bit of criticism. (2000, 210)

In general terms I advocate a collaborative, participative, flexible approach. But we may be ahead of ourselves. Before you declare support for a certain management style, you need to be sure you know your natural style—how you perform now. It's probably worth some time to think about this, and even ask some of your confidants how they perceive you. Once you have a clear sense of your default style, you can examine other alternatives more accurately, and experiment with different methods as situations arise.

It's time to start building your management foundation. Convert the concepts you have learned here into a successful management approach. Show your new team that you know how you want to proceed and that you have the tools to get the job done. Approach your new management position with enthusiasm, confidence, and a solid approach.

Chapter Tips

- Good managers come in all shapes and sizes, but they share certain characteristics. Strong analytical, communications, and people skills are important.
- Management requires an appropriate level of organizational knowledge and activity.
- The terms manager and leader are not synonymous, although good managers strive to be leaders.
- Today's changing workforce is receptive to participative management.

CHAPTER 2

ORGANIZATIONAL MISSION AND VISION PROVIDE A FOUNDATION FOR BUILDING STRATEGY

In this chapter we will discuss establishment and the refinement of a sound strategy that aligns with mission and vision. You need to get in sync with your new boss and with your team about the strategy you are pursuing. It's important to quickly learn your boss's priorities and to convey to your team what those priorities will be.

When you consider how to manage a business organization, everything starts with, and flows from, your organization's mission and vision. This is fundamental because we have already said management is about guiding the organization to produce the right outputs and outcomes. Without awareness of your mission and vision, you can't ensure that you are producing *the right outputs and outcomes.*

The mission is your "reason for being." When I worked at the Department of Veterans Affairs, it was hard to miss a statement that's embedded in the wall at the entrance to VA headquarters. It is a quote from Abraham Lincoln's second inaugural address: "To care for him who shall have borne the battle, and for his widow, and his orphan." This is a clear statement of purpose—a mission. From this type of mission statement your vision and strategy on how to achieve the goal can emerge.

Not every organization has its mission statement stamped at their front entrance. Nonetheless, they all have a mission, usually one that frames their outputs and outcomes for success. Because it's so basic, and so important, every employee should be made aware of the organization's mission and needs to understand how their work group contributes to it. Even more, they need to know how their own efforts fit into the overall picture. This will help them focus on their work and take pride in it. Employees' understanding of mission will also help them appreciate the work being done by other staffers. Supervisors and managers need to regularly frame their work discussions in terms of mission success.

You will know you're on the right path when your employees embrace the mission and actively take pride in doing a job that moves the organization closer to the mission's success.

Your vision is a picture, a description of what your final result will look like, and how you intend to go about achieving that end result.

James A. Belasco put it well in his book *Teaching the Elephant to Dance*: "An empowering vision spells out clearly what you want and inspires people to produce it. A vision specifies a mutual destination— the place everyone agrees to go—and the major activities that get you there" (1990, 99).

Your vision is also used to characterize the kind of organization you want to have. Your organization can emphasize efficiency (keep the costs down); quality (do it right the first time); or customer service (offer the best shopping experience). You can also choose to focus on one or two of several other operating traits, such as growth or increasing market share. But you can't focus on fifty different traits to represent your organizational vision. If you do, you will diffuse your energy and confuse your employees. (They will ask, "Do you want me to do it fast, or do you want me to take time to do it right?")

Mike Krzyzewski offered a solid set of qualities in his book:

"There are also five fundamental qualities that make every team great: communication, trust, collective responsibility, caring, and pride. I like to think of each as a separate finger on the fist. Any one individually is important. But all of them together are unbeatable" (2000, 71).

It's important to give considerable thought to your vision. It can shape the way you organize your staff and your offices. It will affect the way you build your systems. Finally, it will help you design your employee training and mold the way your employees look at their work.

But a vision statement will only help if you use it—if you "live" it. You can't simply write up a glitzy statement and hang it on the wall—or even worse, put it in a file somewhere. Keep your organization's vision statement in mind every day, and consider how it can guide your management actions on a regular basis.

An example may illustrate the importance of vision. The Honda Corporation was started in 1946 as a small company that built engines for motorbikes. Making engines and improving them was their core competence. Over the years Honda has grown enormously and become far more sophisticated, but they have remained true to their core competence and to their commitment (as shown in their company responsibility statement) to be responsible members of their community.

Certainly, adherence to their core competence and their company responsibility statement—their vision—guided their efforts in improving auto emissions. In the 1970s California and the Environmental Protection Agency legislated new emission control standards for automobiles in an attempt to improve air quality. Virtually every carmaker reacted in the same way. They put a catalytic converter on their engines to capture bad emissions. This improved air quality but caused engine performance to diminish.

Honda did not simply add a catalytic converter to their engines. They redesigned their engines to perform more efficiently and produce less harmful emission. They knew who they were; they understood their core competence and it guided their choices. As a result, in 1972 Honda announced the CVCC (compound vortex-combustion controlled), the first engine technology to meet US Clean Air Act standards without the need for a catalytic converter. In 1974 they introduced the first car to meet this standard solely through engine performance: the 1975 Honda Civic CVCC.

So your mission and vision are guideposts for your operation. They clearly post for you what you do, why you exist, where you are going, what you hope to achieve, and how you intend to get there. Without them you will be just wandering in the dark, like Alice, in Wonderland. Alice's lack of vision is shown in her exchange with the Cheshire Cat. It becomes clear that to have a successful journey, you must know where you want to go!

> Alice is in Wonderland and she encounters a fork in the road. She is not sure which route to take. The Cheshire Cat is sitting in a tree at that spot.
>
> "Would you tell me please, which way I ought to go from here," said Alice.
>
> "That depends a good deal on where you want to get to," said the cat.
>
> "I don't much care where … so long as I get somewhere," said Alice.
>
> "Then it doesn't matter which way you go," said the cat.

So let's not be like Alice. She would not have been a good manager.

I had a personal experience a few years ago that illustrates this point. I was leading a discussion with a small group of MPA (master of public administration) students. We were discussing the importance of mission and vision and tying those concepts to individual jobs. A student asked what you do if you have a position with work outputs that do not relate to the mission and vision. After brief discussion among the group it was evident they were confused by this possible circumstance. Ultimately, I told them the affected work team needed to reevaluate the tasks of the affected individual. To the extent the person's work did not contribute to the organization's mission and vision, they were wasting time and resources. The organization could not afford, and should not tolerate, wasted efforts.

Use your organization's mission and vision to help you determine what areas deserve priority. You will need to know how your work element contributes to fulfillment of the corporate mission and vision. For instance, you must understand who you rely on outside of your element and which element(s) rely on you for their success. Without this understanding and awareness you may not be contributing optimally or even satisfactorily to the overall success of your organization. Conduct periodic assessments to determine where your work element is most successfully contributing and where you may have some catching up to do.

In discussions with your boss, your peers, and your direct reports, you should regularly relate your ideas and concerns back to the mission and vision. Doing this will frame the discussions in the right way and will remind your colleagues of the need to always use mission and vision as your guides.

Your mission and vision will also affect the way you structure your operations. You want to be organized in a way that facilitates your vision. If customer service and responsiveness are key parts of your vision, that will guide you in how you set up functions and distribute resources. In designing your workflow, you need to make sure you move output forward in the ways that most effectively accomplish the mission. So take care in how you build your operation's architecture. Make sure your structure facilitates accomplishment of your mission and vision.

As already stated, your strategy flows from the mission and vision. They will help you set your course—what you will do, what kind of organization you will be, and how you will develop into your desired mature organization. With these two key concepts in hand, you can develop a strategy.

A strategy is an action plan. Establishing a strategy involves converting mission and vision into long-range goals and objectives. It includes adoption of courses of action and allocation of resources. The strategy involves description of specific tasks and the priority given to those tasks. Every employee in the organization should be familiar with the corporate strategy, and they should know how their own work and work products contribute to a successful strategy.

When I became the director of the VA regional office in Detroit, that office was structured in traditional arrangement, with divisions for each business line (disability compensation, education, loans, and vocational rehabilitation). Performance varied from one division to another, and overall performance was in the midrange of all regional offices.

I decided to reorganize into small, functional teams. Each team had a clear focus, and they were encouraged to take ownership of their function. For example, one team handled rating evaluation. They were responsible for evaluating disability claims once all necessary evidence had been received. Their primary work product was the formal rating evaluation decision that would be the basis for paying benefits. I asked this team (and all the other functional teams) to recommend team performance metrics and goals.

I met with the team (and all the other teams as well) every quarter to discuss performance, resource issues, and other obstacles. At each meeting we would determine whether the team's performance warranted any reward.

My intent in this reorganization was to get every employee actively involved in strategy execution. I wanted to establish a clear expectation of outputs and priorities for every team and every employee. The new strategy worked quite well. Performance improved across the regional office, some areas showing as much as 40 percent improvement. Employees felt included. They understood what was expected of them.

When you assume your role as a manager, you need to address the issue of strategy. It may be that your organization has already set out a clear strategy. If that is true, you need to learn about corporate strategy. Find out how the strategy was formulated, what big issues it intends to address, and what role your work group is expected to play in executing the strategy. After that you need to review your team's status and confirm that you are actively and productively pursuing the strategy.

As you learn about how your team is addressing the corporate strategy, you need to discuss these activities with your new boss. Get his or her description of the corporate strategy and how he or she describes his team's strategy. Make sure you understand how the boss sees you and your team fitting into the strategic picture. Make sure he or she is aware of your team's activities and endorses them. And make sure you know what outputs and outcomes are most important and plan to regularly update him or her.

Your relationship with your new boss is arguably the most important one you will have in your new position. Your success is tied to him or her. Your boss's impressions of you and your management actions will ultimately influence the organization's impressions of your management efforts, so get in contact with your new boss very early. Get a clear understanding of your responsibilities, any special assignments that will fall under your purview, and priorities of the boss. Solicit his or her opinion on your operations, performance, and staff. Learn what the boss sees as top priorities and highest areas of risk. You need to quickly reach a common understanding of all these areas. You need to find out how, when, and how frequently the boss wants to be updated. You need to stay in close contact.

You may not be so lucky as to inherit a staff that has a clear sense of their role in executing the corporate strategy. Your team's role may be ill-defined. If this is the type of situation you inherited, you have considerable work to do.

A normal part of assuming a new management position is expecting to conduct an environmental scan of your organization to obtain critical baseline information. A general discussion of this process is provided in the next section. If you have found that your team does not understand the strategy they should be executing, your baseline review needs to include a special emphasis on strategic considerations so that you can construct a strategy for the team.

Your interviews with stakeholders and representative customers should include inquiries about how these people view your team's strategic performance. Your review of performance data should include an assessment of the areas where your team has been productively supporting the corporate strategy but its performance has not contributed as clearly to the corporate goals. You should solicit feedback from your staff about where problems may exist or where they have felt out of sync with the rest of the organization.

Also, it is important that you learn about your organization's published strategy. Ultimately, any strategy that you describe for your team must be consistent with, and meld into, the overall strategy of the organization.

Once you have the results of your baseline review in hand, you need to use the information to construct a strategy customized to your team, which will probably involve a discussion with your new team to ensure that everyone has the same understanding of the corporate strategy. You will also need to reach an agreement with your team about how your efforts will support the corporate strategy and how your outputs feed into its overall fulfillment. Hopefully, in the course of these initial discussions, it will become clear where you need to strengthen your performance.

As an example of how this discussion may play out, you may find that your staff produces an output that is passed to other staff and provides the basis for important corporate output. The timeliness and precision of this output is important. You may further discover that your staff is unaware of the critical nature of their own output, and they may not be devoting the appropriate energy and focus to that output. As your discussion with your staff unfolds, you can present this example and have them help you develop better ways to produce and validate the critical output. You should make it clear to your team that you see this effort as important. It will frame the work you do and the way you approach your efforts. It will also reset your relationship with your bosses and other teams.

It may be appropriate to hold a couple of meetings to review the mission and vision and allow for suggestions to refine or update them. This will help frame the strategy development effort and put everyone in a common mind-set.

Your strategic development effort should flow from the organization's mission and vision, as well as a common understanding of what you mean by strategy.

There are hundreds of definitions for strategy and strategy development in management literature. I like the one described here: "The determination of long-range goals and objectives of an enterprise, and the adoption of courses of action and allocation of resources necessary for carrying out these goals" (Bolman and Deal 2003, 62).

The key components of Bolman and Deal's definition are

(1) setting goals and objectives;
(2) adopting specific action plans; and
(3) allocating necessary resources to achieve the goals.

Starting from this platform, have your team discuss in broad terms where you see your group fitting into the overall organization; what outputs and outcomes you produce that are important for organization success. Then build from that into statements of goals and objectives that will help your team more effectively support the organizational strategy.

The goals and objectives you describe for your team should reflect the priorities of the corporate strategy. They should describe tasks that will enhance your group's effectiveness and streamline your operations so they will better support overall strategic efforts.

As part of your annual budget and planning exercise, you should identify new tasks that will take your work group to the next level of effectiveness and organizational support.

As you conduct this budget and planning review, it's important that you identify each of your staff's positions and confirm how they support the corporate strategy. This is the right time to nail down for each position and each person how their work links directly to the mission, vision, and strategy. Doing this will highlight the importance of everyone's individual contribution, and engender a sense of pride in their efforts.

All of this effort should produce a sense of shared commitment and teamwork. You want your staff to feel and act like a team. Including them in a strategy development effort will show that you value their views and that you don't intend to be heavy handed and authoritarian in your approach. They will buy into the strategy once they've contributed. When they are vested in common goals and understand their mutual dependencies, they are likely to work with greater determination. Also, they will be more likely to be cooperative and supportive of your management actions.

It's important to note that involving your team in strategy development, and encouraging their views, does not diminish your authority. As the leader of the group, you retain final say and decision making. However, by being inclusive, you show that you are confident in your role, that you value staff recommendations, and that the team's results will be better for the collaboration.

"People want to be on a team. They want to be part of something bigger than themselves. They want to be in a situation where they feel that they are doing something for the greater good" (Krzyzewski 2000, 185).

Lawler also addresses this issue:

> Perhaps the most direct relationship between motivation and participation occurs when people participate in setting goals and commit themselves to

achieving these goals. According to research, when people participate in setting goals and get information about their performance two things happen. First, they set goals that are perceived by them to be achievable. Second, their sense of self-esteem and competence becomes tied to achieving the goals and therefore they are highly motivated to achieve them. (1986, 30)

As you go about setting strategy for your team, make sure you stay in close communication with your boss. You need his or her support, and you want his or her advice, input, and validation of your efforts. The last thing you want is to project an image of a maverick, running loose and setting your own direction.

Chapter Tips

- Building a strong relationship with your new boss is critical. Start working on that right away.
- Work with your new team to clarify and develop the ways they will contribute to organizational strategy execution.

CHAPTER 3
SETTING UP YOUR SPACE

Properly setting up your office space is important, and in this chapter we will talk about appropriate steps to ensure maximum efficiency. It's important that you review your space, work tools, and other resources to learn where you have sufficient resources and where you might need to shore up.

When you initially assume your new management position, you may not have a lot of latitude in determining your physical layout. It's likely you will inherit existing space from your predecessor. Within the parameters you are given, you should consider how you want to operate. If your new office is in a remote spot, and you want to be more centralized to your staff's locations, maybe you can rearrange the existing layout so that you are closer to the action. Conversely, if you prefer a quiet environment and your given space is in the middle of everything, you should consider some rearrangements, and quickly. You will rapidly become immersed in daily activities and dealing with your new responsibilities. You deserve a comfortable environment, and you will function better if you have one. So don't resign yourself to a physical situation that will frustrate you.

The physical proximity of your secretary or administrative assistant is important. If you will rely heavily on this person for managing the flow of daily activities, you want him or her near you. If you need substantial time for concentrated reading or analysis, you may need your assistant to monitor the flow of people and work to your space.

If you don't inherit the tools necessary to conduct your work, you'll need to identify your needs early and submit the appropriate requests. In doing this assessment, talk with your staff. Get their feelings about any operational needs that have been problematic or ignored.

If you determine that changes in workflow are needed, you should work with staff to make necessary revisions. You will need to remind your staff of the desired outputs at each stage and then demonstrate why you believe the changes will be helpful and how they should enhance the process. This requires you to be knowledgeable about the work processes.

Mike Krzyzewski said, "A leader has to work through the process with them so that he *knows* they will perform their jobs well during a game. You can't just tell people what to do and then expect them to perform well" (2000, 89).

Almost every office maintains a formal organizational chart that shows how authority flows through the organization. It should reflect who reports to whom and where indirect, informal linkages exist. You need to review the chart and determine whether it reflects current reality, or if changes have evolved over time without corresponding updates to the formal chart.

Let your staff know of your intent to review the organizational structure. Invite their input. Let them know you have no preconceived notions about changing the structure. Your interest is in gaining understanding and acting to streamline relationships wherever possible.

Annotate any revisions. Once again, talk with staff to confirm what the real operating structure is. If any reporting lines do not appear logical, find out the history behind them and what issues those reporting lines were intended to improve.

On initial review, you will expect to see a logical flow of authority. Hopefully there will be reasonably consistent distribution of authority across the organization so that managers and executives of similar rank have similar control. Where you observe apparent unevenness, you should examine the situation(s) further. It may be that changes have been made over time and that these changes have successfully addressed problems. Regardless, you need to learn the reasoning behind the structure. You also need to decide whether to continue the special circumstances or direct adjustments that will still address the historical issues while simplifying the overall picture.

It's possible that the circumstances that initially caused problems and necessitated the special circumstances disappeared long ago. If so, it will be important to decide whether continuation of the special circumstances is warranted.

Look at the cost associated with your current operating structure. Your goal is to operate at maximum efficiency. You want to know that the structure is as streamlined as possible. The number of procedural steps in your processes should be minimized to the extent that the people involved in a single work process should be centralized. Alternatively, you can link your work group electronically and create a virtual collocation. This simplifies progression through the processes and minimizes delays between steps.

There can be benefits in simplifying work processes so that personnel and operating costs can be reduced. But sometimes you can be more efficient by consolidating steps and giving employees more latitude to handle larger parts of the overall processes. You will have to assess the differences and make choices as to which way to build out your operation.

In reviewing how your team's operations were constructed, consider how well that structure facilitates production of your desired outputs. Hopefully your organization is arranged in a way that promotes fast and efficient production of your outputs. This structure—your organizational architecture—should have been designed with deliberation in order to reduce steps and time and get the job done as effectively as possible. It may be that your organizational architecture has really been constructed with duct tape and bubble gum. You need to know if you are leveraging technology to improve outputs, or if your work processes have been shoehorned to fit into existing systems.

Many organizations go through periodic modernizations. As the business world changes and operating tools become more advanced, opportunities to streamline operations occur, so it makes sense to do periodic revisions. As you begin at your new organization, you can benefit from examining the most recent modernizations to learn what the perceived vulnerabilities were at the time of the latest revision, and what new tools were expected to facilitate improvements. Then you can compare the theory of that modernization to the reality of the current operations structure and workflows. You should probe into the areas where you see variance between theory and reality.

Hopefully, review of the most recent modernization efforts will enlighten you about what was considered to be the most effective organizational architecture and why. Use this information to engage your staff in discussions about your organizational architecture. If structural improvements are needed, you want to begin that process as soon as possible. As with other areas in your initial review, you need to listen to the advice of your staff, involve them in design of any structural changes, and get them to buy into the revisions you ultimately propose.

You need to get baseline information about your new operation, which is like getting a report card on the organization. Talk with people who are knowledgeable about your team, including top management, and representatives from sister units (other staffs that work on areas that intersect or overlap with yours) that feed your team inputs or to whom your group submits products. Review any written documentation that describes your unit's purpose and responsibilities. Examine data reports and any ad hoc analyses that have been done to assess the performance of your unit.

The purpose of gathering and reviewing this baseline information is to give you a starting point for your work. You need to know the strengths and weaknesses of your operation. You need to know where actions flow smoothly and productively. You also need to know where the stresses—mechanical and emotional—exist.

As you look for this material, you may find some do not exist. There may be no formal charter for your operation, for example, but somehow your work responsibilities have evolved and been defined for your unit. You may find documentation for your operations lacking, and then you have an opportunity and obligation to correct that deficiency and establish formal guiding principles.

This is a good thing. It gives you the opportunity to recalibrate elements of your operation and requires you to coordinate with sister staffs and your boss, so that all parties agree on what you are responsible for producing.

Gathering this baseline information will flow from the environmental scan you conducted to confirm your operation's strategic role in the organization. This data gathering will cascade down to the nuts and bolts of your operation.

The level of funding your office receives, and how that funding is authorized, is important. You need to quickly learn the budget: overall funding levels, where the funds have been distributed within your organization, and whether there are any contingencies on any of the funds. You will want to know whether your funding levels have been stable in recent years or were vacillating upward or downward.

It is probably wise to request briefing(s) on the office budget very quickly after your arrival. You can ask your managers to present briefings on their allocations without making suggestions. Encourage them to offer opinions on high points and potential issues, so they give you their sense of how well the current budget meets their needs.

Look for anomalies in this opening budget review. If one account is receiving a higher percentage of total funds than you would normally expect, find out why your new organization values the area so much. If another account seems to be underfunded, do the same type of analysis. If these anomalies are adequately explained, let your staff know you accept them. If you're uncomfortable with the explanations, dig deeper. Let your staff know you remain skeptical. Ultimately, if you cannot reconcile the variance, adjust those budgetary allocations with the caveat that you will welcome appeals. This will demonstrate fairness and a commitment to an open process.

You need to find out how your new office develops and tracks their budget. You need to get comfortable with the data, so let your analysts know how you like the data presented. Also, set up regular briefings at intervals that suit your needs. By doing this, you let your staff know how important the budget is to you.

If you will be given a seat at the table when resources are allocated, you need to know how to prepare for those sessions and maximize your distribution. If you are not directly involved in the budget allocation decisions, you need to be an advocate for your staff with the manager who represents you in the allocation process (probably your boss). You should provide your budget representative with information that supports your budget request and relates resources directly to the strategic tasks for which you are responsible.

You should also make sure that someone on your staff has clear responsibility for monitoring expenditures and developing estimates on future resource requests. You should schedule regular meetings with this person and meet as often as you need to maintain your comfort level with the budget. Let your representative know where your greatest interests are and how you want to see the data presented. This will make your discussions more productive.

Find out how the operation is perceived both internally and externally. To do this, you should talk with top management; listen to their characterization of your new operation. Find out whether they think your group is high performing. Learn where there have been issues in the recent past. Probe them for the strengths and weaknesses of your personnel.

You should learn about your office's relationships with other internal staffs. Where strong dependencies exist, has your staff been productive and cooperative? It is important to know if there are any interoffice rivalries or jealousies because those conditions will almost certainly have a negative effect on productivity. If you can identify such rivalries early, you can solicit causes and potential solutions from affected staff when they are most likely to open up about the issues. If time passes and these jealousies persist, people will begin to perceive that the status quo will not change (and is even supported) by your team.

You should seek information about the operation's priorities. What tasks or assignments have they been given? Are ongoing projects progressing satisfactorily? Discover any historical problems in any areas.

You should talk with your staff in group settings and individually. They certainly have opinions—some may be held very strongly—about what's right and what's wrong with your organization. Early in your tenure is the best time to solicit these opinions. It's important that you not disclose the sources of negative feedback and that you offer attribution for positive ideas you intend to implement. This is one of several ways to build trust.

Learn what top management sees as top priorities and how your group plays a part in fulfilling those priorities. Hopefully you will find documentation that describes the role they are expected to play in strategic deployment. If that documentation is not available, you will need to seek it through interviews and discussions with your boss and management colleagues, as discussed above.

If your group is pursuing projects to upgrade process methodologies or streamline operations, you should review and validate these efforts. Make sure you can support the direction these projects are taking as well as the budget allocations provided to each one. Direct any necessary adjustments early, so disruption is minimized and your desires are made known.

It is also appropriate to ask your boss and other executives how your new organization is perceived around the rest of the company. You will want to learn about performance trends for your shop but also about your reputation for collaboration and cooperation with other offices. You can also benefit from hearing about any historical issues that have affected your organization. If one or more significant issues have arisen, you need to know about them. You should also inquire as to whether those issues have been eliminated, resolved, or incorporated into standard operations.

When you talk with executives about your new organization, try to learn how they see your group fitting into the overall operation and the corporate strategy. Hopefully, you will get consistent responses that will help solidify your view of your team. If you hear variations and inconsistent replies, you will have clues to pursue and resolve those variant views.

You should learn the background behind the three to five tasks that occupy the greatest part of your resources on an ongoing basis. How did these work projects evolve, and how was your operation given jurisdiction over the projects? Find out whether the situations that led to establishment of these key tasks still exist. Ask yourself whether these few key tasks are still viable and providing value to the corporation. If answers to these questions are unclear, you may have an early opportunity to realign your work operations and redistribute your resources.

As you work through your baseline review, you should publish an initial set of administrative policies that you intend to use. This should at least address such basic matters as office conduct, work-from-home options, and vacation and leave rules. You should highlight any administrative policies that are being changed or reemphasized, with some associated explanation regarding the basis for the changes. Areas where the status quo is being retained should also be included in this publication, so there is as much clarity as possible.

At the same time you should identify and publicize any initial priorities that you intend to pursue, as well as any operational changes you intend to make. Your baseline review will certainly identify areas where improvement is warranted. Your staff will be acutely aware that you have been conducting the review. Publicly and quickly identifying new priorities and operational changes will help settle anxieties arising from uncertainty.

As you announce these first steps, it's appropriate to offer rationale. You don't want to come across as arbitrary with your first significant actions. Referring to the advice you may have received in your review, or the current inefficiencies of certain operations, will provide context for your decisions and hopefully will resonate with the staff.

As you establish these new priorities, you need to resource them. Set up appropriate work teams. Provide initial expectations and corresponding resources. Where possible, identify the performance indicators you intend to track. Offer the new teams opportunity to do their own quick review of the project and make recommendations for adjustments.

Chapter Tips

- Consider rearranging existing space to improve your operational utility.
- Conduct an early review of your budget process so you know where you have adequate resources and where you may need to pursue additional funding.
- Do an analysis to determine your operational baseline. What's working well? Where do you need to make improvements?
- Discuss your findings with your boss to ensure you both see these issues the same way.

CHAPTER 4
MAKING INITIAL OPERATIONAL CHOICES

I n this chapter we will look at some of the informal elements of
your work environment and how you should examine them at the
outset of your tenure. These areas include the character, or culture, of
your work group; the controlling authorities, or delegations, for doing
business; and the manner in which your team communicates with
your office and with each other.

Work groups that function over significant time exhibit behaviors
and attitudes. Collectively, these constitute the culture of the work
group. A group's culture can be robust and positive. When it is, it
supports a positive work environment. A group's culture can also sour
over time. When this happens, when negativism grows, it will likely
adversely affect the group's performance. So it's important to assess
the culture of your new office very early in your tenure.

Don't underestimate the importance of culture. Belasco used a real
example to make this point:

> Every organization has a culture that shapes behavior.
> Sometimes the culture works for you. Culture worked
> for Johnson & Johnson when it hit the Tylenol

[poisoning] crises in 1982 and 1985. When news of the problem came in, managers used the company vision to make decisions. The company's vision states (in part), "We believe our first responsibility is to the doctors, nurses, and patients, to mothers and all other who use our products and services ... We are responsible to the communities in which we live and work and to the world as well." Using these statements as empowerers of their behavior, Johnson & Johnson managers recalled every package from every shelf in the world. Managers were applauded for taking responsibility and the dramatic short-term financial loss. (1990, 202)

You want to know how your office operates on a day-to-day basis. Do the people interact informally? Is there a lot of interoffice communication? Are there social groups or activities that create different relationships than those in the formal structure? These arrangements can be productive. They can generate friendships that can facilitate resolution of issues that arise.

The activities can also be detrimental. If the social activities are allowed to overlap too heavily into office hours, those activities can result in reduced productivity.

Another aspect of the office culture is the manner of communications. On one end of the spectrum, your office could operate rather formally. Senior executives might be addressed as Mr. or Ms. Hotshot. Attempts to drop in on colleagues without an appointment might be frowned upon. Meetings are normally scheduled formally and in advance.

On the other end of the spectrum, your office might operate very informally. It might be common and accepted practice to walk unannounced into your colleague's office to discuss an issue. You might refer to your bosses by their first names, and they might encourage "fly-bys" (where you poke your head inside someone's office to ask a quick question or address an issue) or direct phone calls to discuss issues without clearing through a secretary.

Wherever your office falls on the formality scale, the key is whether that mode is effective. As long as the authority of managers and executives is respected, it may be productive for them to be informal and accessible to the staff.

You need to make some judgments on what you will permit and where the lines between work and social activities should be drawn. My preference is for a reasonable amount of socialization to be encouraged. It's easier to work with people if you are comfortable with them. Getting to know your colleagues on a social level will probably lead to more collaborative behavior and less suspicion of each other's motives. For a very simple example, if you are having trouble getting needed input from another office, and if you have a good, informal relationship with Joe from that office, then you are more likely to pick up the phone and call him to discuss the matter. Joe will be more amenable to working through the issue and less likely to become defensive than if he received an impersonal memo from a stranger.

As you set up operations, you should offer guidance on behavior and expectations. Your staff deserves to understand what you expect from them. Having said that, I do not suggest you build a rule-bound organization. You want your team to understand their roles and expectations. You should not try to describe every detail of their activities. Mike Krzyzewski said: "Too many rules get in the way of leadership. They just put you in a box and, sooner or later, a rule-happy leader will wind up in a situation where he wants to use some discretion but is forced to go along with some decree that he himself has concocted" (2000, 10).

Krzyzewski continues:

> Well, if you're always striving to achieve a success that
> is defined by someone else, I think you'll always be

frustrated. There will never be enough championships. There will never be enough wins. And when you finally attain them, if you're lucky enough to do so, they'll only be numbers. Somebody will say you were great or that you were successful, but ultimately you'll know it's an empty success. (2000, 54)

While you are structuring your organization to be effective, you want to be sure people know where they have been granted authority to act. Look at the existing documentation on this. Hopefully there is a manual or file that documents any ongoing delegations of authority.

Review the existing delegations to understand them and to gain insight into how the organization has evolved. You need to be comfortable with the level of delegations, so if there are areas you don't understand the reasoning for a delegation or are initially uncomfortable with it, discuss it with your team. As part of your initial review, you may consider having all materials come through you for a cycle or two so you can learn the workflow and see how things have been getting done. After you complete your analysis, you should share your conclusions with your team. If changes are contemplated, you should explain why you are considering making the changes. If certain delegations are to be eliminated, you should explain those.

Remember that when you announce these changes, you are setting policy. You are making a statement about the way you want the organization to look. If your delegation changes are generally more restrictive, you are telling the staff you want to tighten up. That's okay; it may be the appropriate step. However, this decision will likely sensitize your staff. They have probably grown comfortable with the current arrangements. They may feel diminished that they now have to get approval for (what they consider) routine actions. So be careful with the tone you set.

If you choose to restrict authority because you think the organization is chaotic and out of control, you should advise the staff that you have concerns and explain how you think existing practices have hampered effectiveness. Tie your concerns to performance issues. Let them know the delegations will be reviewed periodically, and where the team demonstrates growth and responsibility, expanded delegations will be reconsidered.

In the end these issues revolve around business issues. If delegations make the team operate more effectively, they should be endorsed. If delegations have resulted in more mistakes, or inconsistency in procedures, they should be considered for tightening up.

Over time, as you get to know your staff and build trust with them, you will probably want to expand delegations. Proper use of this tool expands your overall capacity and streamlines processes. As Wess Roberts wrote in *Leadership Secrets of Attila the Hun*: "A chieftain should allow his subordinates the privilege of making decisions appropriate to their level of responsibility. Weak is the chieftain who reserves every decision for himself out of fear that he might lose control" (1985, 67).

An example of this process occurred when I moved into the position of chief, field operations for the VA education program. In early discussions with my new team, a couple of the senior analysts offered to handle the scheduling of audits to help relieve my new workload. Upon reflection, I decided that the audit scheduling was a core function of my position. Through proper scheduling I could ensure that audits were rotated properly among the staff, and that every office received audits at expected intervals. So I declined my staff's generous offer and looked for other areas to offload work.

As we have already discussed, your work unit must be aware of, and aligned with, the corporate strategy. The main outputs that your work unit produces should contribute to the accomplishment of corporate strategic priorities. Your staff should have an understanding of how their work products feed the corporate strategy. If your staff is expending significant energy on outputs that cannot be linked to the corporate strategy, then those processes and outputs should be critically reviewed. Your team may be producing the shiniest, coolest widgets in the world, but if those widgets don't contribute to the organization's desired outcomes, the widgets are worthless.

An important component of your initial review should involve learning how your organization has been conducting strategic planning and whether they've had cyclical, scheduled reviews of those plans. You must also find out your organization's strategic role. Were they active participants in developing strategic plans for the entire organization or passive recipients of strategic choices made by the executives above you?

Your staff has hopefully been involved in strategic development discussions. If they have been afforded the opportunity to provide input, and if their views have been incorporated in the global plans, the likelihood of their buy-in is greater. Conversely, if they have been excluded from strategic planning efforts, you will need to ensure that they understand the strategy and accept it as their own. If this is not the case, you will have to spend time and effort building acceptance for the corporate plans.

Ensuring strategic alignment must be one of your earliest efforts. Every day that passes with your team being strategically misaligned results in wasted effort and reduced effectiveness. So explain your team's role in the corporate strategy, and work through any confusion or frustration. Give everyone a chance to voice their concerns. The goal of this exercise must be to gain consensus on your strategic alignment. Do not move on until that is achieved.

Communications is very important to an organization, and an effective communications network does not occur magically. It requires work. As the manager, you have to encourage the type of communications you want on your team. You need to model the style you wish to promote. You also need to make it clear what business information needs to be shared from individual to individual or subgroup to subgroup.

If one subgroup needs to pass product to another unit on a

recurring basis, it may be helpful for them to let the receiving group know when new batches are being released. More pertinently, the sending group needs to let the receiving group know when unusual circumstances cause changes to their delivery times. If the groups are working on very short time lines, it probably won't be as productive to communicate through e-mail. A telephone call between you and your colleague will get you the needed information on a more timely basis.

Communications among your staff members should be fluid and productive. Staff should be comfortable communicating with each other in a variety of ways—face-to-face, telephone, text, and the like. Individual staff members should be clear and comfortable with their lines of communication with bosses, peers, and subordinates. There should be avenues for regular, structured discussions of business activities.

If your team members are reluctant to talk about business items among themselves, you may need to create situations where success will depend on effective discussions among team members. An example would be to direct a small group (of reluctant communicators) to jointly prepare a presentation; you could include a condition that each member must give part of the presentation. Then leave it to them to work out the details.

Having said that, I must add one important caveat:

Good communications does not equal more meetings!

In my experience, organizations demand that their managers spend a lot of time in meetings. While there are good reasons to conduct meetings (e.g., to discuss strategies, performance reviews, etc.), you will increase productivity if you limit their number and duration. No one in a meeting is producing anything. So when you schedule a meeting, be sure you know the purpose and feel comfortable that it's the right avenue to accomplish your purpose. Then hold to a very tight schedule. The shorter the better. Generally, meetings that extend beyond an hour lose focus and waste time.

It will be helpful to know how your predecessor was perceived as a communicator.

I generally favor an open and informal style of communication, but your organization may be used to a different style—maybe a little formal and structured. Before you jump in and make dramatic changes, make a determination on how effectively the current mechanism is operating. As a new incumbent you will have numerous opportunities for making change. If you have an effective communications network in place, it probably will be advantageous to use it. You can integrate stylistic changes over time, but your most important initial concern will be getting your new message out clearly. Don't unnecessarily increase discomfort.

Let's try to make this point more clearly by constructing an example. Suppose you are a new manager who has inherited a very effective organization. Your organization is accustomed to a top-down communications network. The previous boss was very much a command-and-control practitioner. He spent a lot of time developing assignments and tasks; he directed what work was to be done, by whom, and in what ways.

Your staff became accustomed to this style and are performing well. You have a preference for a more collaborative approach, with open give-and-take discussions about assignments. Give your staff latitude to develop the know-how to do projects. It would be risky to come into this organization and dictate a significant and abrupt change of approach. You would probably raise anxiety and undergo an extensive period of diminished efficiency while your staff grows into your preferred method.

In this scenario the new manager should take it upon himself or herself to absorb the discomfort and allow the organization to continue its operating approach, at least for the short term. It would be appropriate to advise your new staff of your preferences, and you could selectively test out your approach on volunteers and new projects. You would have opportunities to guide the staff through initial attempts. You could develop it further as people's comfort levels increased.

For some people and some tasks, you may wish to continue the traditional approach because they showed clear discomfort with the change and their current performance is excellent.

Also, you need to think about how you present to your staff. You can be the figure of authority; you can impress the staff with your technical knowledge and use that as the base for discussions with them.

But if you rely heavily on your own judgment, portraying yourself as highly confident in your analytical abilities and unlikely to admit mistakes, your staff will react accordingly. They may become reluctant to offer ideas because you always present your own as the preferred direction. They will not offer criticisms or alternatives because you will choose your own ideas anyway. And when you do make a logical or analytical mistake, you can bet your life the staff will take great joy in sharing that around the break room.

Instead of presenting as some all-knowing authority, there's much to be gained by being a little humble. Be quick to admit that you don't know something or don't have experience in a certain area. Welcome ideas, recognize the special expertise of various staff members, and openly accept criticisms of your ideas. If you can do this, your people will open up to you. They will gain confidence, engage more willingly in discussions about differing approaches, and respect your authority more. They will see that you are confident in your role and with your limitations. They will come to understand that you are about finding the best way to do business, and you will more readily find the best ways if you are open to new ideas.

What you communicate is as important as your communication style. You need to find a common ground with your boss. After you have completed your environmental scan, you should meet with him or her to discuss your impressions. Give your observations about what seems to be working right and where there is room for improvement.

Indicate the work areas and performance indicators that appear to require the most attention.

During initial meetings with your boss, you need to solicit his or her feedback. Listen to his or her version of the good, the bad, and the ugly. In the end, the areas that are most important to your boss are those that will be most important to you too. Because you are looking at the organization with fresh eyes, you're likely to interpret things a little differently. If you have concerns about items that have not been sensitive to your boss and the team, you should press those areas. Trust your analysis. Don't give up on your issues until you're satisfied that your first impressions can be explained and perhaps mitigated by factors you might not have noted.

Ultimately, one of your important goals with the boss is to find common ground and context for ongoing business discussions. You will need to learn how the boss views different issues, how he or she analyzes them, and what data he or she likes to use. This is important because you will be far more comfortable and successful if you can get on the same wavelength with your boss (use terminology he or she is comfortable with; refer to data that he or she uses and trusts). If that means you will be translating data and terminology for yourself, so be it. Simplifying things for your boss is part of your job, and a little extra interpretation for your needs is the cost.

So you want to align your communications with your boss.

In communicating with the boss, you need to defer to his or her preferences. If you try to insist on approaches and data that you are most comfortable with, even when the boss is not comfortable with those things, you will waste time and probably risk losing credibility until you convert your approach to his or hers.

As you are working to establish good communications with your boss, you also need to establish effective communications with your subordinates. It would likely be helpful to let them know what analytical tools, data elements, and performance measures you encountered in your initial analysis that were novel or confusing. You should also share your tendencies in relaying business information. Your staff absolutely needs to know what you discover about your boss's preferences and priorities, as well as how you intend to frame business issues for him or her.

In the same way you must adapt to your boss's needs for information, your staff needs to do that for you. You can make their adaptation easier by being forthcoming in explaining the approaches and data that you will want to see and use.

All your work to build strong, effective communications will serve to strengthen organizational alignment, or line of sight, up and down the organization.

Chapter Tips

- Learning about the existing culture of your team will help you in shaping how you proceed in any reorganizing you undertake.
- Delegations should be reviewed early on. Get background where needed, and let staff know quickly about any changes you plan to make.
- Defer to your boss's style and data presentation preferences. If comfortable with your interactions, he or she will be more receptive to your ideas.

CHAPTER 5
ENSURING YOU HAVE THE RIGHT
SYSTEMS AND RESOURCES IN PLACE

In this chapter we will discuss the importance of organizational alignment, or line of sight. These concepts refer to the need to have systems and processes designed effectively so that work flows smoothly and efficiently and so employees can see how their work outputs contribute to the organization's mission and vision. All employees should understand why their outputs are important and how they contribute to organizational success. We will also talk about relationships with sister staffs and creating a sense of shared fate with those staffs.

The chapter includes discussion about the value in learning about the people on your staff, what's important to them, and what motivates them. Further, there is review of the need for developmental training for staff members to ensure their professional growth. We will also discuss the need to review staffing and equipment needs early on.

You will need to be sure that all employees know what their functions are, who they receive work from, and to whom and where they send outputs. As you review data and talk with people, probe into whether they feel their work and outputs are valued. It is important for employees to know how their work contributes to the organization.

Knowing what the core outputs are is important; understanding why those outputs are critical to organizational success is huge.

If you find that your new organization does not have clear organizational alignment, or that your staff has a low level of consciousness about the concept, you will have to raise their understanding by linking the initial management moves you make to improvement in line of sight. You should take time to explain how your first round of changes is intended to streamline operations and improve line of sight.

Even if you choose not to make early changes, you should explain why you feel the current arrangement is effective. You should take time to show the team how you see signs of good organizational alignment; how key outputs are treated with priority; and how outputs from each area are being moved swiftly and effectively to the next production stage. This is a terrific opportunity to let your new staff know you are impressed with the operating procedures and systems they have developed and that you appreciate their efforts. Be liberal in passing out credit.

You need to build in your staff a sense of ownership of the work and pride in what they are doing. It's important to reinforce their partnership with their peers so that they know they are all contributing positively to the jointly desired outcomes.

Edward Lawler addresses this issue:

> First, when individuals feel responsible for their tasks, they seem to be much more motivated to turn out a high-quality product than they were before. Second, as they gain a broader perspective on the entire product or service, they can often catch errors that might have gone undetected due to lack of knowledge. In short, they get a broader perspective on the work and, as a result, can do it better. (1986, 92)

Obviously, for job enrichment to succeed, the individuals must be capable of adding to their skills and abilities and be motivated by such intrinsic rewards as a sense of accomplishment, achievement, and competence. (1986, 95)

You will need to review and confirm the inputs and stimuli for your operation. These are the raw materials you use to produce your outputs; the actions that cause your organization to initiate a process of work; the timing for those inputs. Obtaining this information will probably involve an examination of your organization's workflow and some discussion with colleagues on the staffs that provide inputs to your staff. You will need to learn about the inputs to your work processes; where those inputs originate; why they are prepared a certain way for delivery to you; and how those inputs have evolved over time.

Certainly, you will want to learn about how the people involved in these inputting processes feel about their operation and their relationship with your staff. If the working relationship between your staff and the inputting staff has been strong and positive, then that will offer a robust foundation for you. If there have been tensions or issues between the two staffs, then you will have an early opportunity to make improvements in that work relationship. Indeed, you will have a responsibility to review the causes of tension in the relationship and make some adjustments, so you demonstrate a commitment to a strong and productive relationship.

Let's discuss an example to show how the relationship between you and your inputting staffs can have significant effects on your work. Suppose you work in a factory that makes school desks. Your team is responsible for receiving rough-cut desktop pieces and sanding them down so the edges are ready to be painted.

The work group that feeds your team the desktops has quotas to meet, so they quickly push their work along. When they hurry, they often cut rougher edges, which requires more work from and time spent by your staff.

You need to talk with your inputting staff chief colleague and let him or her know how the nature of his or her product affects your work. Your colleague may very well sympathize but decline to change his or her work process because of his or her quotas. But if you could agree on a mechanism that would vest his or her team in the production of your team (for example, they get incentives to help your team increase your production) and sell that to your joint boss, then everyone wins. And if you do this, your colleague will immediately have an increased interest in your production and your needs.

Confirm that you have the right resources to do the work, including personnel and other resources. The tools your people use to accomplish their work are very important; the people themselves are arguably your most valuable resource. Those people need to be treated like a valuable resource—that means they need to be appreciated, cared for, and fully developed. The earlier you can convey that message, the better. If you act in a way that makes your team members feel valued, it will pay great dividends. Conversely, if you take your people for granted, act like they're only doing what's expected, and you only give feedback when things go wrong, you will get the type of employees you deserve—unhappy and unproductive ones.

Get to know the people who work for you. Learn what drives them, what makes them tick. You could make a strong argument that a boss should not try to get to know his or her employees beyond their business role, that they should keep things completely focused on the work and not get complicated by the various elements in their employees' lives. I don't care how strong you can make the argument; I disagree with and dismiss it. Everyone deals with a variety of factors that drive their behavior and attitude toward work. Some employees have special physical or mental issues that can greatly affect what they can do and how they do it. You need to learn about the special conditions that drive your staff. It can be helpful for you to know about the priorities people have outside the office.

You need to accommodate special needs and priorities and will benefit from taking a compassionate attitude toward them. This doesn't mean you must diminish expectations for everyone who is dealing with issues. Rather, it means that if you, as the boss, acknowledge that almost everyone is dealing with various issues outside their workplace, and that if you can help them address those outside issues, they will be more comfortable at work. They will focus better and be loyal to you, a fair and reasonable person who cares about them.

You must be sure your people have the skills to do their work. Check their educational backgrounds; look into organizational records for formal and on-the-job training. Check to see if new staff orientation is provided so they have clear initial guidance about what is expected, how they will execute their processes, where the necessary directives reside, and how to get questions resolved.

The scope of developmental training offered by your organization is closely related to the existing credentials and skills of your staff members. You hope to find training curricula that offer progression from novice to journeyman level in key positions. If such programs do exist, it is important to find out how effective they are and how they are perceived by staff. If you cannot find evidence of this type of developmental training, such opportunities should be given priority.

Support of a robust training program is important, and your early actions to support training will send a powerful message. If you do not take the time to analyze this area early in your tenure, you certainly will find yourself scrambling to react when you suddenly find yourself with a significant training need. Make the necessary time early to assess your employee development program, and direct any necessary enhancements, so you are ready to meet your employees' needs as they arise.

You should do an initial review of your staffing levels. You will want to know how appropriate staffing levels have been determined.

Look for efficiency studies, or time and motion studies (which involve observation of a task using a timekeeping device to ascertain the time required to do the given task) that have estimated necessary man-hours for each task. If no such assessments are available, you should inquire about how staffing levels have been established.

You should look into the types of equipment your staff is using to do their work. Ideally, you will be using state-of-the-art equipment at each operating stage. At a minimum, your people should have equipment and work tools that allow them to complete their work efficiently, without delays or extra steps. If you find deficiencies, you should talk with your team and find out why the work tools have not been upgraded. Then, explore how the team members feel you should go about upgrading equipment. With that information, you should determine the most expeditious way to bring the equipment up to a reasonable, usable level.

As discussed in chapter 3, you need to learn about the budget allocation process in your organization to quickly make sure you are in control. This topic relates closely to the discussion above, on strategic alignment. Your work processes must produce the right outputs and outcomes for the organization and must be routed to the right place. This might sound extremely basic and unnecessary, but it should not be overlooked.

Everyone in an organization should understand how their work product contributes to the overall strategy and successful outcomes. This needs to be confirmed, but more analysis should be done as well. Things have a way of mysteriously changing. When your operations were set up, or when they last underwent systematic review, an assessment was likely done to make certain that each operation aligned with and supported strategy. This assessment needs to be repeated periodically to validate that outputs and outcomes remain intact. In daily activities, people make minor adjustments that seem to improve things or remove obstacles, and these minor adjustments add up. Over time they can unwittingly affect the nature of your outputs.

Roberts wrote, "Chieftains grow to understand that the wisdom of a particular decision can change with time. Make every effort, therefore, to improve future decisions by learning from those you've already made" (1985, 69).

Chapter Tips

- People are your most important resource; treat them with great care.
- Learn how staffing levels have been determined. Become a strong advocate for acceptable staffing levels and the right tools and equipment.

CHAPTER 6
PERFORMANCE OVERSIGHT;
MEASURING THE RIGHT STUFF

E very organization needs reliable, objective oversight. You need the right performance measures in place to inform you about the effectiveness of your operation. If you have the right measures, you need the right oversight process to review results and make corrections where necessary. You need to openly review the existing oversight processes, solicit staff inputs, and demonstrate a commitment to fairness.

For Belasco, this is about expectations. He said the following:

If you don't expect it—and tell your people you want it—you'll never get it. People are very poor mind readers.

- *Set specific, numeric expectations.* People are motivated to achieve things they can see, touch, and measure. Imagine bowling if you couldn't see how many pins you knocked over. My guess is you'd soon get bored with the game and quit. Expect specific numeric outcomes and accept nothing less.
- *Stand firm.* You'll get the argument "I agree with you, but quantifiable goals are just not possible in this situation" The giants in the management studies field all disagree. Professors

> N. Edward Deming, George Odiorne, and Peter Drucker
> argue that all management activities can be measured.
> Read the following pages and see for yourself. I believe that
> every management situation can be measured in one of
> four quantitative terms—units, money, time, and customer
> satisfaction. (1990, 152)

Everyone understands that oversight is necessary, but too often it is an area that suffers because it's discomforting. Reviewing work outputs is fundamental and is one of the most basic ways you can minimize risks and maximize potential for success. Every component of your operation must be subjected to oversight, not just the main work process that generates your primary outputs. You need oversight of support functions, purchasing, budgeting, training, and so on.

In your initial assessment, you need to confirm that oversight protocols exist for every component of your section. You should satisfy yourself that quality control reviews are set up at proper stages of the operations and that procedures are in place to eliminate defects without adversely affecting other elements. You should confirm that the person (or position) assigned to perform oversight is a sensible choice given your organizational structure. While the conduct of oversight review is important, you need to satisfy yourself that the oversight activity is not eating up too many of your resources. Like everything else in the organization, oversight needs to be efficient.

An important part of this assessment is to find out how your organization has been rewarding success. You need to get a sense of how the performance evaluation and reward process is perceived by staff. If your performance measures are seen as valid and fair, they will be given respect and attention. If they are seen a biased and unfair, staff will view them with reluctance and skepticism. If rewards are meaningful and clearly linked to accomplishment, then the rewards will be valued and respected. What key performance measures do they track? Can you see how those measures fairly and objectively track progress? Do you see any gaps in what they have been measuring? Given their existing measures, how have they been performing? It's important to note that the way you measure and report on performance should be motivating to the organization and not be perceived as a negative.

It is probably appropriate to talk with supervisors and staff about the performance measurement process. Solicit opinions about the objectivity of the measures and their use by previous management. You need to learn how goal-level performance marks have been set (if they have been set) and about performance variances among various staffs and individuals. You should consider changes to the performance management system early. If you review it and let it stand without changes, it will appear as if you endorse the prior system.

If you are lucky, you will inherit a performance management system that is already in place and perceived to have value. If so, you still need to review performance data, familiarize yourself with the information, and recommend any amendments. You should try to retain as much of the existing system as is practical because it is trusted and valued by your staff.

If you inherit a performance system that is not valued or used, you must quickly act to make changes. You need the system to be meaningful. In this situation, start from the basic outputs and outcomes that your operation generates. Assemble key performance elements that will allow you to track production volume, timeliness, quality, and any other components, such as customer satisfaction.

Discuss performance measurement with your staff. Find out what they think is important and why. As you revise the process, make sure to gather performance elements that relate to each person's function. Be sure they are producing the right outputs for you. They need to understand that their outputs are important to the overall success.

Throughout this evaluation, you want to send the clear message that performance management is important. It is a key tool to make sure you are moving in the right direction. You want your staff to know

you want a system that is fair, objective, and transparent. You should not back away from the fact that performance reviews will be used to identify deficiencies both organizationally and individually. But you need to be very clear that it is about improving performance, not about gotchas.

As Lawler said:

> Unless individuals perceive that the behavior or performance that leads to a valued reward is achievable, they will not be motivated to perform. Thus an organization may clearly tie a number of very positive rewards to a particular level to performance and still find that individuals are not motivated to perform at that level simply because they do not perceive that they can achieve the performance. (1986, 29)

As you review performance metrics and consider changes, you need to adhere to some fundamental characteristics. The performance metrics you use should be fair and objective; they should relate directly to your key outputs and outcomes; the metrics should be easy to compile directly from performance systems; the data should be public and accessible to everyone.

If you miss the mark in this area, it will hinder your efforts to track your progress. If people perceive your new, revised system to be distorted or biased, they will quickly lose interest. If your new metrics are compiled by a series of artificial calculations rather than gathered directly from production systems, their value will be diminished—and people's perception of them will become jaded.

Your effort to validate and even enhance the performance management system is important. People are sensitive to this area and your changes will be subjected to close scrutiny. This doesn't give you an excuse to waive the effort. Rather, it highlights the need to proceed carefully, solicit input from your direct reports and your boss, and to assure yourself that at the end you have performance metrics

that reflect the key outputs and outcomes of your staff, and that the data is compiled directly from production data and is not subject to distortion.

You will need to listen closely to the feedback you get on your prospective changes to performance metrics. Satisfy yourself that the new metrics are good and fair, and that you have incorporated suggestions where you could. When you are ready to start using the new metrics, you should do so publicly—letting your staff know, and assuring them that if any of the new metrics don't work out, you will review them again. Throughout this process you need to act as—and be seen as—the promoter of a good, fair performance management system who is open-minded, and focused on management improvement.

In all the above areas—top management's opinion of your staff, how well your staff has been addressing top management's priorities, where and how well your staff melds with the rest of the organization, and whether the staff is using the right performance measures to gauge their performance—time is critical to the incoming manager. If you present to the staff as objective, fair, willing to consider new ideas, and solely focused on improving operations, people will be likely to share their thoughts and concerns with you.

If you act quickly on at least some of the inputs you receive, people will take note. Hopefully, they will conclude that you really do want to improve operations, and that is your only motivation.

If you quickly settle in to an operations management approach, without doing an exhaustive assessment and looking for staff ideas on how to improve, the staff is highly likely to conclude that you have accepted the status quo and are unlikely to change the things that concern them. They will probably hunker down and become reluctant to open up about these issues.

Chapter Tips

- Let your staff know your feelings about performance measurement and your approach to it.
- Conduct your initial performance measurement review openly; solicit staff views. Demonstrate a commitment to fair and objective oversight.

CHAPTER 7
DAY-TO-DAY OPERATIONS; KEEPING THEM GOING

Once you have done your baseline operational review and made some preliminary decisions about operations, you have essentially set up shop. You have critiqued the organization; you have made some declarations about areas of perceived deficiencies (as well as strength); you have ordered some changes. But you haven't yet established how you will conduct business on a day-to-day basis. So that's next on the agenda.

To recap: You need to organize yourself. You should know how you operate most effectively, so you want to set up staffing structure and workflow that fits your style. Talk with your immediate staff. Let them know what you are trying to achieve and how you want materials presented to you. You need to clearly lay out the information (reports, correspondence, etc.) that you want to see on a regular basis. You also need to be clear about the materials you want handled by staff. Based on your initial review, you should have validated existing delegations or made adjustments to them. You can change them if things don't work out based on initial assignments, and it probably will be appropriate to review delegations again in six to nine months. By then you will have meaningful experience with them.

Talk with your immediate staff about their roles. The people who you inherited in your front office, those who work closely around you, will have some of the same anxieties the rest of your staff had when you arrived. They will notice that you brought some new people with you. They likely thought they were doing a good job but now are concerned about whether their position will be retained, reshaped, or replaced. It seems new bosses often come in and review the big picture but ignore the people and operations closest to them.

You should directly and quickly address these concerns. The faster you can get people into comfort mode, the faster you will dissipate their anxieties.

Your office should be set up to address the same basic operational components as those you examined when starting up:

- strategic alignment
- inputs
- systems/organizational architecture
- continuous communication
- performance and progress measurement
- resource utilization and development
- line of sight
- outputs
- oversight

In addition to these components, you need to build in capacity to consider and develop operational improvements.

Your day-to-day activities should be geared to monitoring the basic components of the organization and removing production obstacles as they emerge; identifying and correcting flaws or variances that may insinuate into the workflows; and making systemic improvements where opportunities arise. You need to continually verify that resources are properly distributed and focused appropriately. Recruitment delays or complications with equipment purchases can significantly hinder your effectiveness. Systems reliability and availability can also be a major influence, so they must constantly be observed. You will receive new directives from upper management and will need to take necessary steps to incorporate these directives into your operations.

When you entered your managerial position, you reviewed the corporate strategy and satisfied yourself that your work unit was properly aligned. This same type of review must be done periodically to ensure your ongoing alignment with corporate strategy. Actions taken by your bosses will inevitably affect the organization's strategy. Changes in law or in marketplace interests will require that you make appropriate adjustments to your strategy. You need to make sure you are consciously aware of the evolving, unexpected conditions that influence your ongoing activities, and you must make the appropriate adjustments in your approach so that your work unit continues to contribute to strategic execution.

As you observe these strategic effects, you should devise adjustments to your processes and discuss them with your boss to ensure that he or she agrees. Your boss may have already identified the strategic activities. You will need to discuss your observations, proposed task, and final conclusions about what management reactions were appropriate. You need to stay consistent with him or her and make sure you are not diverging from his or her intentions.

You need to be confident that your operation is receiving input from other areas in a timely and efficient manner. You should have standards for timely receipt of work items; you should have procedures in place that describe where your inputs are to be received and in what format. Your staff should know where and when to feed this information into operations. Build a cooperative relationship with your counterparts on any inputting staffs. Have regular discussions to notify each other of changes. This way you will be able to minimize occurrences that could negatively affect staff. If you share ideas for improving each operation, you may find additional opportunities for joint innovations.

There should be quality controls in place that monitor your system inputs. These quality controls should assess whether the inputs are flowing into your work queues effectively, and whether they are accurate and correctly formatted. You should receive assessments from the quality control element at regular intervals, and these assessments should inform you about the timing, quality, and formatting of the system inputs.

The structure and staffing of these quality control elements should be discussed and accepted by all staff involved in the cross-staff functions. Everyone needs to buy into the process. If any team member feels left out, or that the process is biased against him or her, resentment will build.

You need to address fluctuations in the input processing as you observe them. If you see that system inputs are getting to your group later and later, you need to communicate that to your colleagues. You should jointly analyze the causes of the delays and make procedural corrections as necessary. These findings and system corrections should be noted in a quality control log for future reference. If the delay types recur from time to time, it is an indicator of more serious problems, and this should trigger a broader and more rigorous systemic review.

As you observe input fluctuations and consider making procedural corrections, you need to be in contact with your colleagues on the inputting staff(s). Find out if they knew about the fluctuations and if there are resource issues that could be causing them. It may be that the corrective action needs to be taken by the sister staff. You need to be communicative and supportive and confident that intended corrections do not complicate the efforts of another staff.

At the input stage of your work process, as in all work stages, you need to periodically reassure yourself that your staff is functioning effectively. You must check to see that your people are following standard procedure. If tweaks or informal enhancements have been injected into the process, you need to review them to ascertain what generated the enhancements. You must ensure that they truly enhance the process and that no unforeseen effects are creeping into the process. You can accomplish this through a combination of actions—your daily reviews and discussions with staff may bring issues to light, or your periodic systematic analyses should catch them.

Correct handling of efforts by your staff to make informal process enhancements is extremely important. You will want to encourage creativity and innovation. They are closest to the work and most likely to identify flaws or offer enhancements.

However, you don't want this done chaotically, so you need a process for review and approval of innovative proposals. Such a process is important for system controls, but it cannot be tedious or it will stifle the innovations. You should build a simple way for workers to offer suggestions. You should assign clear responsibility for review; a timely, meaningful process should be put into place. You need to set a tone that innovative thinking is desirable and will be acknowledged.

When a suggestion for process enhancement sounds good, you will want to support it. Look for ways to implement the suggestions or to prototype them, if that's more appropriate. Applauding innovative thinking without trying out the ideas is hollow praise.

The attitude of supporting change, and of encouraging ideas from the ranks, will almost certainly yield positive results. People will feel empowered and encouraged that their ideas are given real credibility. Many large and profitable companies experience bear this out—notably, Toyota. Toyota's support of innovation among their line employees is described elaborately in *The Elegant Solution* by Matthew E. May.

Peters and Waterman advocate a strong policy toward people and their ideas:

> Treat people as adults. Treat them as partners; treat them with dignity; treat them with respect. Treat *them*—not capital spending and automation—as the primary source of productivity gains. These are fundamental lessons from the excellent companies

research. In other words, if you want productivity and the financial reward that goes with it, you must treat your workers as your most important asset. In *A Business and Its Beliefs*, Thomas J. Watson Jr. puts it well: "IBM's philosophy is largely contained in three simple beliefs. I want to begin with what I think is the most important: our respect for the individual. This is a simple concept, but in IBM it occupies a major portion of management time. We devote more effort to it than anything else. This belief was bone-deep in my father." (1982, 238)

Champions are pioneers, and pioneers get shot at. The companies that get the most from champions, therefore, are those that have rich support networks so their pioneers will flourish. This point is so important it's hard to overstress. No support systems, no champions. No champions, no innovations.

What strikes us most about the excellent companies is the completeness of their support systems for champions. In fact, the excellent companies are structured to create champions. In particular, their systems are designed to "leak" so that scrounging champions can get something done. (1982, 211)

Of course this issue of creativity melded with systemic processes spans well beyond the input phase of your operations. It applies to all phases of your operation. Your encouragement of innovation and insistence on systemic rigor must cascade through all areas of your work.

As mentioned above, your organizational framework, or operations architecture, should be built around the purpose served by the organization. This means your workflow systems, your technological systems, and your people systems should be organized in a way that is consistent with your mission and vision. If your vision is that you will be a customer-oriented business, your systems should be set up to maximize customer service. You may need a substantial cadre of customer service representatives to interact with the customer, and you will need to provide that customer service cadre with the tools needed to offer good service. If your vision focuses on efficiency or cost reduction, you may organize with less support functions staff (in support areas like customer response) and instead focus your energy on building the production system that builds your outputs in the most efficient way. You may determine that you want to automate more of your work processes to save personnel costs (be careful, as automation does not always save money).

Make efforts to have your production systems reflect your vision of the kind of organization you want. If you want your organization to be characterized by a certain approach, your operating systems need to reflect that. This process is an evolving one. You will make initial decisions on how to construct your operation. Then you should observe the operation in practice because it is likely that some aspects of your systems will clearly reflect your vision. Other aspects may not execute as intended, and because of that they will not reflect your vision. So you refine the process.

Remember that systems are built to help you generate your desired outputs and outcomes. The systems themselves are tools, not outcomes. It's easy to get swept away with glitzy tools, but the tools only have value if they facilitate the creation of your real, intended outcomes.

Building your work systems the right way will facilitate having a clear line of sight throughout your team, and you need to ensure that everyone in your organization has a clear line of sight from their work to the ultimate outcomes of the organization. Hopefully, when you first came into your management position, you checked this and made any adjustments needed to clarify the staff alignment.

Like anything else, your team's line of sight can get distorted over time. You need to periodically check. Make sure the work is being performed according to directives and if there are any new people in the operations. If so, do they clearly understand why their work outputs are instrumental to overall success? Confirm that these new people understand why a certain presentation of their outputs is important. A regular schedule of systematic analyses is needed to guarantee proper reviews are done.

You need to ensure that your veteran staffers still understand their roles and that they have not become jaded or discouraged. If there is discouragement, you will need to run down the causes and make necessary changes to restore balance.

While you are reviewing and confirming the clarity of organizational alignment throughout the organization, you should also look for ways to improve the operations. Talk with your direct labor staff; ask them what works and what doesn't. Look for ways to streamline operations in ways that will clarify your line of sight and shorten the path from start to finish. Of course, as always, if you decide to make operational changes, test them out first and document them.

Line of sight can be clarified by visual reminders throughout your operation. You should look for posters, signs, and any other appropriate methods to remind your staff of the ultimate products you produce and the customers you serve. Ideally, images will show *what* you produce and *why* your products have *value*. Such reminders can instill pride, based on the reminder that they are doing good work and producing valued products. Recommended reading on this topic is Stewart Liff's 2007 book *Seeing Is Believing: How the New Art of Visual Management Can Boost Performance Throughout Your Organization.* Visual management techniques can be quite helpful in building the right environment.

Clearly, resources play an important role in successful execution of your strategy and production of your expected outputs and outcomes. In your organization's budget process, you (or your predecessor) probably submitted a resource request. Hopefully it reflected your prudent view of the number of people and funds necessary to produce your expected outputs and outcomes. As budget decisions were made, you received your allocation, probably some amount less than your request. Hopefully you had an opportunity to adjust your output expectations based on the lesser funding level.

Unfortunately, your bosses may feel that a 5 percent reduction in funding does not translate into a 5 percent reduction in outputs. So you may be challenged to produce some higher portion of the fully funded operation. Make your best case; accept what you are ultimately given and expected to produce. Then, adapt your staffing and your architecture to maximize your effectiveness.

In terms of your day-to-day management activities, you need to regularly review your overall resource allocation and the distribution of those resources.

Make sure you are sustaining a full staffing level (the full amount you have been authorized). Sometimes, as people come and go through your organization, delays can occur that keep you at less than full staffing. Similarly, while you probably directed funding levels for the various staff elements and initiatives, the flow of those funding levels can get delayed or diverted for any number of reasons. In your day-to-day reviews, you need to be watchful of these distortions and take corrective actions to put resource dedication back into proper perspective.

You need to be tuned in to your operations every day. You need to keep yourself apprised of the workflows, systems reliability, and consistent production. Regularly check the pulse of your operations. Everything might have been going fine yesterday, but it only takes one problem to cause things to move out of control.

Check with your people on a regular basis and whether they are feeling stressed or are dealing with operational problems. The first step is awareness. Only if you stay in touch with your operations can you accurately determine whether you should intervene on an issue or if your team is productively working through the problems. You don't want to jump into every issue. You want your staff to learn and grow confident by working through issues, but you must also be ready to assist if a problem becomes critical or seems particularly vexing.

Keeping the right balance between awareness, encouragement, and direct intervention is part of the art of management. In the eyes of your staff, there is a fine line between productive, proactive management and micromanagement. If they see you as a micromanager, they will resent your involvement. If they feel that you are removed from their operations, they are likely to conclude you either don't know what's going on or don't care. You need to successfully walk that tightrope.

Check your numbers. See if the number of outputs remains consistent. If you see spikes, look deeper for the causes. Talk with your staff to see if anything has changed and whether changes are having unforeseen results. Often, there are small adjustments made that go unnoticed in day-to-day activities. These adjustments deserve attention. They deserve scrutiny to ensure against unexpected results.

When big changes occur, everyone is generally aware, but this is not enough. You need to evaluate the influence of the big changes and eliminate any bad results. You also need to publicize the big changes to let people know about them and why they are being endorsed or revised.

Regularly validate the accuracy or precision of your outputs. You must be confident that outputs are being finished according to specification and with regularity and reliability. As with anything else, if you find that precision is too low or is varying unacceptably, you need to review the situation and look for causes.

Review your unit's timeliness or productivity. You may find that you are producing the right volume of outputs. You may also see that the accuracy of production is good. But you also need to confirm that the amount of time and energy taken to produce outputs is good.

Obviously, it would not be good to find that you have had to double staff allocation in order to maintain an acceptable production level, so if any element of your operation is demanding increased resources to maintain production levels, you need to look into why. It may be that something has altered the production mix and that prior expectations need to be revised to accommodate the new reality. On the other hand, it may be that workflows have been unintentionally distorted and caused inefficiencies. Either way, you need to be aware of changes to productivity levels and take the appropriate steps to continue maximized efficiency. You may need to adjust expectations if operational circumstances have been permanently altered.

This discussion leads to the conclusion that you should establish a series of operational/systematic analyses to review all significant operations or workflows. Any significant operation that directly affects your output or outcome production needs to be analyzed periodically. You should schedule frequent analyses for those systems that have previously shown the most volatility and those that have the greatest bearing on outcome production. The sequence and frequency of these reviews should be determined by you.

In conducting reviews, try to work with your subordinate supervisors. Be careful not to jump past them (undermine them) to direct corrective actions. You need to trust them and give them a chance to make necessary adjustments. If you see conditions that do not appear to be getting attention, you need to act. But your first step should be to see if your supervisors are aware and taking action. By checking with them first, you build trust and partnership. You also let them know you are indeed watching in a productive way—not looking for gotchas—and you haven't lost your analytical skills.

The joy and frustration of managing activities is that things never seem to be permanently fixed. A major part of your job is to keep your hand on the pulse of the organization, so you can quickly identify and address new issues. You don't want new production problems or complications to get a foothold and begin to expand. You need to identify, assess, and fix the emerging problems as fast as possible so they don't get a chance to significantly affect production.

The fact that nothing is permanently fixed and new complications can emerge without warning demands that managers be flexible. This is why oversight processes are so critical. There need to be adequate systems checks in place to notice any new variables that might require attention. You, the manager, or your designees need to be constantly vigilant in looking for the new wrinkles that could grow and distort production if left untreated. If you allow your oversight activities to diminish, it is almost certain that problems will multiply, and the costs of fixing these new problems will quickly outgrow the costs of an efficient oversight program. Don't let your oversight process be strictly about finding problems. Make sure you spend a fair amount of energy finding new solutions. Every problem is also an opportunity to make an innovative change that will significantly enhance your production. In your team's problem analysis, there should be consideration about whether the problematic operation needs reengineering.

When you are established in your position, you should have confirmed or made changes to the rewards system. You should have a mechanism for periodic (annually, quarterly, etc.) formal recognition of superior performance. You should be able to see which individuals and units are producing above expectations. Your rewards system should provide for public recognition of this superior performance.

The rewards that you offer need to be meaningful. That doesn't mean they need to be extravagant or outrageous. Rather, it means the rewards need to fit the performance achievements and should reflect consistent appreciation from one performance period to another. The evaluation process should accurately identify superior accomplishments, and the rewards should reflect sincere appreciation by management. That probably sounds overly simple, but my experience is that failure to maintain these fundamental characteristics seems pretty common.

For example, your reward system will quickly lose credibility if you recognize the wrong people. If the person who receives the highest reward is generally known to take credit for others' work, your system will immediately lose credibility. Second, if your reward system generates significant monetary awards, but receipt of the rewards is accompanied by critical or demeaning comments by the bosses (e.g., "I'm surprised to see Epley is receiving another award"). Thirdly, if you—as the boss—don't participate in the rewards dissemination, it probably will send the message that you don't endorse the results.

Fairness, objectivity, and sincerity are important in any rewards process. The reward criteria need to be transparent and tied to specific, tangible achievements. They should reflect the business realities of your world. If your unit had a good year, rewards should be plentiful. If your teams had a difficult time meeting performance expectations, the rewards should reflect that—but, even in bad years, there are good performers who need to be acknowledged.

Chapter Tips

- Organize yourself. Create an office structure and workflow that improve your efficiency.
- Regularly review your strategy implementation and alignment so you don't allow variances to grow.
- Make sure your operational architecture supports your purpose.
- Maintain a broad-based system of oversight analyses.
- Validate and revise your rewards system to ensure its credibility.

CHAPTER 8
STAYING IN TOUCH WITH YOUR BOSS

One of the most important people in our work life is the boss. In this chapter we will discuss that special relationship and offer insights into how you can positively influence the way you interact with your boss.

The boss sets priorities, assigns work, criticizes, praises, and evaluates your performance. The boss recommends you for pay increases and opportunities for promotions and more responsibility. With all these levers at his or her disposal, it becomes important to your work satisfaction that you earn the boss's respect and keep him or her satisfied about your areas of responsibility.

You must understand and accept that the boss has the power in your relationship. You must accede to whatever he or she needs. To do that, you must learn what drives the boss, how information is best received, and what is expected from you and your team. You need to adapt your style to the boss's.

Some basic steps can help you build a strong relationship.

You need to know what your areas of responsibility will be. As mentioned in chapter 2, you should have gotten initial, general statements of expectations, including priorities and any special assignments in your earliest conversations with your boss. As soon as you have reviewed your job description, assignments, and summarized early conversations with the boss, you should have confirming talks with the boss to clearly delineate your responsibilities. You and the boss need to have clear, common understanding of your role.

Your boss has responsibility for executing some portion of the corporate strategy. You, in turn, have responsibility for executing strategic assignments for the work in your area. Some of this work will be ongoing in nature; it will represent a core portion of your work. You will also (almost certainly) have ad hoc assignments geared to promote the corporate strategy. You need to get in sync and stay in sync with your boss about these tasks. Get clear statements of expectations from the boss: what is expected for each strategic task; when deliverables are due; how he or she wishes to receive updates.

You need to keep the strategic tasks moving forward and determine that no distortions occur. If, as you manage these tasks, you see that your efforts may be affecting other aspects of the business, you must alert your boss. You should have done adequate analysis to allow you to offer suggestions on adapting to the unforeseen results.

You have a responsibility for making sure your outputs on strategic efforts feed directly to the appropriate place in the organization and that the form of your deliverable is acceptable to the receiving office.

Discuss your initial impressions with your boss about organizational architecture. If you found that your group's procedures are outdated and respond to antiquated problems, you need to let the boss know. You should ask for his or her confirmation that your findings are valid and get his or her approval for your proposed changes. If the boss can provide additional background information that explains why the current procedures still have value, you need to hear that as early as possible.

If you end up implementing changes to improve the line of sight, you need to ensure that your boss supports your intentions. People have a way of getting comfortable with the status quo whether it's efficient or not. Special relationships sometimes form that cause things to flow better in spite of a weak design. Your boss is likely to know of these special circumstances and can advise accordingly. Failure to get your boss's support can be wasteful and costly. It could even cause you to back out your new and "better" processes when the boss sees them and tells you why the old way was better.

You need to learn how to communicate effectively with the boss. Does he or she prefer regular one-on-one discussions; does he prefer written summaries of activities or "fly-bys"? You need to adapt to his or her preferences and use them to provide updates.

You owe the boss good work and good assignment updates so that he or she is comfortable with all areas you are working on. With that as a given, it is in your best interest to stay ahead of the game. You need to keep him or her informed on all aspects of our work *before* he or she has questions or concerns. Nobody likes to be blindsided, and that means no surprises for the boss. If there are problems with an assignment, you need to inform the boss before he or she hears about it elsewhere. When you inform about a problem, you should have thought about it enough to offer some assessment—you think you have a resource deficiency, one of your suppliers has been habitually late, and so forth. If you need the boss's assistance, you need to be prepared to describe how he or she can help, and quantify your needs.

All this implies that you need to train your boss to receive and discuss your updates in a regular fashion—comfortable to him or her, and "doable" for you. If you want to provide written summaries, find the venue he or she likes—spreadsheets, narrative summaries, and the like. For verbal updates, find the time and the place that works for him or her so he or she is comfortable and receptive.

You need to learn how to read cues from the boss. When he or she is becoming critical of a task, how does he or she react? How does he or she tend to convey irritation with an issue? When you see those signs, you need to "talk him or her down"—let him or her know that you will do an assessment of the issue and report to him. Quickly defusing these issues will help improve your overall relationship.

If issues arise on colleagues' assignments, you need to be careful.

The boss may ask for input, or you may have a stake that allows you to comment, but you need to frame your comments to make it clear your vantage point is as observer or stakeholder, that you don't have access to full information and the involved employee or team will be better positioned to provide full assessment. So you say you have had some delays, and the other project manager is assessing the situation and you will jointly advise the boss by (suggest a date). Or your project team and the other project team have some differences in approach and you could both benefit from the boss's advice—can you set up a joint briefing next week?

Once you get on your boss's wavelength and gain some confidence, you can communicate much more freely. However, even if you get really confident, you must not forget he or she is the boss, so retain appropriate professional demeanor and distance at all times.

You want to be able to influence the boss. When he or she considers or issues directives, you may wish to request some changes. When you have difficulties meeting performance expectations, you need to explain any extraordinary factors and receive adjustments in expectations because of mitigating circumstances. There will be occasions when you need to request additional resources.

When these things happen, you need to request assistance or indulgence from the boss. Your chances will be greatly enhanced if the boss feels that you have built a record of solid performance, that you have prudently used resources, and that you consistently maximize outputs within prescribed constraints. The boss will be more receptive to your requests if he or she believes you do so only when necessary, such as when you have exhausted possible internal adjustments.

You need to earn the reputation with your boss that you are a can-do person. You need to avoid being perceived as a whiner who always seems to need more from the boss.

Keep these thoughts in mind when you interact with your boss:

- He or she can help or hinder you.

- It's your responsibility to nurture the relationship.
- You are the one who must demonstrate a solid record and a clear pattern of maximizing all the resources provided.

It's important to keep the boss apprised on resource utilization. In your recurring meetings, advise the boss on how you have distributed your resources among various projects and ongoing tasks. If limited resource availability has been an issue, emphasize the actions you have taken and how you are balancing the results across all activities. You need to keep the boss satisfied that you are effectively using your resources and that production levels reflect his priorities in all areas.

You will have to make funding and personnel adjustments from time to time. Unforeseen circumstances will demand that you react with appropriate actions. As you make these ongoing corrections, you must keep the boss up to speed and gain his or her acceptance of your revisions.

If you notice that a work area is stressed or requiring more resources than anticipated to sustain acceptable productivity, you need to analyze the situation. Specifically, you need to learn whether the problem is temporary or if it reflects a new, permanent reality that will continue to demand increased resources. If it is permanent, you will need to determine if a reduced level of production is tolerable or if resources must be diverted to sustain the operation. Then you will need to explain the root causes to the boss, along with your proposal to adapt to the new reality. The timing and detail of your reporting should reflect the size and scope of the issue.

Just as you have set up performance measures for your staff, your boss will want to have measures in place for you. One of his or her key responsibilities is to oversee your progress. Embrace this need. Do not hide from it or try to avoid it. Rather, you should get actively involved in the development of your own performance measures. You can and should influence the final measures. You want them to be responsive to the boss's needs, but you also want them to be practical and achievable for yourself. The performance measures that you are assessed on should reflect the core work processes and outputs that your staff works on.

This is a key area in your work life. If your boss is focusing on the things that you think are fundamental in your operation, your relationship with the boss has much higher potential than if he or she is continually looking for progress reports on tangential issues. Keeping the boss updated will not take an inordinate amount of time because you will be reviewing the same information for your own benefit.

Your goal should be to provide your boss the data to satisfy his or her oversight needs while ensuring that the performance data is easily accessible to you. If you feel existing performance measures can be improved, do the necessary analysis to develop alternatives. Then, present the alternatives to your boss, with your explanation regarding why the new version is preferable to both your needs.

Chapter Tips

- Your relationship with your boss is likely the most important one you will develop at work.
- As you do your initial reviews and make operational changes, get the boss's approval. Failure to do so will be wasteful and costly.
- Learn how the boss likes to receive information/data. Adapt to his or her style and stay ahead of the boss on progress updates.
- Work with the boss on developing your performance measures. If possible, make sure your performance measures reflect your core work processes and outputs.

CHAPTER 9
GUIDING YOUR STAFF

In this chapter we will discuss the value of building trust with your staff. This includes being open and consistent in your approach. Building and maintaining open communications with your staff will build a positive environment. We will discuss the importance of giving your staff clear expectations and holding them accountable in an open, objective fashion.

"Managing down" refers to the way you work with, organize, and guide the people who work for you. These are your direct reports and those who report to your direct reports. These employees need several things from you, but one of the most important is *trust*. If they trust you, they will follow your guidance willingly and without hesitation. If they don't, they will always be looking behind your instructions for the hidden agendas; they will be more reticent and less inclined to offer up new ideas. So you need to generate trust.

As Bennis wrote:

> There are four ingredients leaders have that generate
> and sustain trust:
>
> 1. Constancy. Whatever surprises leaders themselves may
>   face, they don't create any for the group. Leaders are all of
>   a piece; they stay the course.

2. Congruity. Leaders walk their talk. In true leaders, there is not gap between the theories they espouse and the life they practice.
3. Reliability. Leaders are there when it counts; they are ready to support their coworkers in the moments that matter.
4. Integrity. Leaders honor their commitments and promises.

When these four factors are in place, people will be on your side. (1985, 160)

Bennis's thoughts are simple and powerful. Your staff will work better and be less stressed if they know how to read you. You want to be transparent and consistent. If your staff understands you in this way, they will gain confidence. They will be less anxious about how you will react to issues and will be more willing and able to take some initiative on those emerging problems. They can anticipate your guidance and act accordingly without waiting for you to deliver the guidance. Your constancy, or consistent approach, is empowering.

Perhaps it needs to be added that while transparent and consistent are good management behaviors, they are not sufficient. These behaviors must be coupled with an objective and compassionate approach. If you have a strong, explosive temper and you go off at the drop of a hat, that would be clear, consistent, and predictable, but it won't get the right results. Your people will spend all their time ducking you and avoiding your tantrums. Work will suffer. Don't do that.

Making sure your actions reflect your stated beliefs is important. It's easy to say you want your staff to act a certain way or to approach issues in a prescribed manner. In practice, there will be times when your beliefs get tested. Some mitigating factor will intervene to test your resolve.

Let's say your boss directs an approach that contradicts your stated policies. Your boss's directive will probably carry the day, but how that transpires is important. If you pointedly but respectfully raise concerns and let him or her know you have some discomfort with the approach because it varies from your ongoing guidance, and if you offer alternatives that are consistent with your own policies, your staff will see consistency. They will see that you stand up for your beliefs. You will be able to explain the ultimate decision to them with a peaceful resolve that you made your case and the boss made his or her choice.

In this type of example it is equally important that your staff sees you implement the boss's choice fully and in the best way you can. There can be no foot-dragging or whining about the decision. You need to show loyalty to your boss before you can expect that same loyalty from your staff.

Another key component of building trust relates to the handling of stress. Business offices all have some measure of stress. After all, the goal is to produce a product fast and with precision and sell it with a maximum profit. This requires concerted effort, and that level of effort can be stressful.

As the manager, you need to effectively handle stress in your office. Most of the time you should be concentrating on diminishing stress levels, allowing your staff to relax and function at maximum efficiency. You need to absorb the stresses as they build to insulate your staff. Do this by removing obstacles, facilitating workflow adjustments as necessary, and so on. Take away the potential distractions that may diminish productivity.

Of course there will be times when you cause increased stress. For example, you may receive an assignment for your team that has a super high priority or a short time line. The circumstances of such an assignment bring their own stresses. Since you can't ignore the stresses, work with them. Be clear with your staff that the new task is important, acknowledging that the deadline is tight. Be supportive at the same time. Remind them that such assignments bring recognition and are opportunities to show their capabilities. Stay involved and keep the team properly focused so the built-in stressors don't take over.

As another example, you may have one or more employees who are not fully pulling their weight. You will need to exert a little (or a lot) of pressure in these instances so the staff understands their responsibility and gives a little extra effort. Even in these circumstances, though, you need to ensure that the pressure to improve remains positively focused on producing your products and the team's success.

It's important that you remain conscious of your role in managing stress. If you do this effectively, your team will be more productive and relaxed. Your more challenged producers may feel some stress, but it will be focused to provide incentive to improve their productivity.

Good managers stay in constant communication with their staff and let them know their expectations. When requirements change, the manager discusses them, with some explanation regarding the impetus for the change.

Peters and Waterman addressed this issue well: "When Ed Carlson was president of United Airlines, he said, 'Nothing is worse for morale than a lack of information down in the ranks. I call it NETMA—nobody ever tells me anything—and I have tried hard to minimize that problem.' Analyst Richard Pascale observes that Carlson 'shared with the field staff confidential daily operation statistics that were previously regarded as too sensitive for the field to handle'" (1982, 267).

This kind of open and relaxed communications will pay dividends. The staff will feel more involved and trusted, and they will become more vested in results.

You are the funnel of information from the corporation to your team. Keep the information flow going steadily and make sure you provide regular updates on all important corporate initiatives. This will contribute to greater buy-in from your team; they will increasingly feel part of the corporate structure, and it will reduce feelings of isolation. This funneling of information includes letting your team know how your bosses are reacting to current team performance as well as how the team is handling issues. It can provide a boost if your team knows their work is getting the attention of the higher-ups.

So keep your staff apprised of all the updates from above. This includes the good, the bad, and the ugly. You communicate the good by letting folks know when the boss is pleased about an item—spread the credit as widely as possible among the staff. Everybody involved with the praiseworthy work element should share the spotlight. Elaborate on the bad, but don't assign blame—at least not publicly. If the boss is disappointed in an output or a recent production trend, let people know that, but frame it as positively as possible ("this is an opportunity for improvement, or this clearly becomes a priority for us"). Sometimes news from the boss transcends bad—it becomes ugly. Don't hide that either. Information has a way of seeping out anyway, usually distorted into an even worse scenario. So share the "ugly" news, but bear the weight of responsibility on your own shoulders: "I acknowledged the deficiency and assured the boss I will redouble my efforts. I will, or course, need your help."

Communications need to be handled using a variety of methods. Depending on the setting, this includes speeches, formal presentations, meetings (keep the number and duration down), memoranda, and performance goals and standards. It also includes more informal methods such as visual reminders and one-on-one discussions. The reason you need to use multiple delivery methods is that everyone hears things and learns differently. If you and I hear the boss give a directive, we are likely to take away slightly different versions of the message. If the boss gives the same directive several times in several venues, it becomes more likely that the core message will be received by everyone.

Policies and priorities gain strength when cited regularly. If, in your discussions with staff, you regularly refer to the same three top priorities, it will sink in that the priorities are real and not going away. This will give comfort to the staff that their efforts are meaningful.

Nothing is more frustrating than a work situation where the boss changes priorities every week.

Policies and directives need to be communicated to everyone affected by them. This seems so evident that it need not be stated— except it's not always done. Devise a system for publishing all significant policies and directives so that everyone knows where they are kept and has access to them. When changes are made, they need to be published as amendments to the earlier policy. This should be communicated verbally as well. It does no good to revise policies if no one knows about them.

If you publish policies or directives that derive from directives of your superiors, you need to make that association clear. You need to make reference to the higher-level directive in your policy statements and show how one is derived from the other. This will reinforce the line of sight throughout the organization. You are not doing business in a vacuum.

Maintaining close communications with your staff also means being available for discussion. You want them to feel comfortable bringing questions to you for resolution. This type of relationship will reduce frustration and allow you to quickly address misinterpretations so they have minimal effect. It will also increase productivity—if people are struggling with confusing instructions, you can resolve this quickly and get people back to work. But if the staff is hesitant to bring these issues to you, the confusion and anxiety—and the reduced production—will persist until you stumble on and resolve it.

You should encourage discussion among your staff. Each person's work overlaps the work of others. They are the experts in their areas. They can and should help each other. People can learn from the experiences of their peers. If this is done routinely, the organization will grow. Individually learned lessons will be shared and diminish struggles for others. The exchange of ideas will bond the staff members more closely.

Your staff will need reminders from time to time about how their roles fit into the corporate picture and understand how their outputs contribute to its overall success.

When you entered your position, you confirmed that your team, individually and collectively, supported the corporate strategy. You reviewed each position to ensure that you and they could see a clear line of sight from their work to the desired corporate outcomes. Sometimes your organization's strategies will change. Conscious decisions will be made to reach your desired outcomes by a different route. For this reason you need to periodically review each work station to reassure that you are optimally supporting the mission. As you conduct these reviews, you need to reassure your staff that their work processes continue to support the strategy—or that their work processes need to be slightly revised to continue optimal effectiveness. Either way, your staff needs and deserves reassurance that their work remains viable. As you engineer changes to operations, you should explain how the new changes will sustain or enhance your organizational alignment.

Another reason for doing these periodic strategy reviews is that work processes and outputs have a way of evolving without conscious effort. Day-to-day activities drive minor adjustments that can add up to significant change over time, so your team's processes and outputs must continue to be as effective as possible.

Keeping this type of context visible and tangible to everyone will help your team function better. If your people know that operational changes are not taking away but are enhancing their core functions, they are less likely to get anxious about the enhancements. It's your job to give them the proper context and keep them comfortable in their roles. You owe it to your people to give them clear expectations. Staff members deserve to know what you expect them to be doing, what outputs are required, and why those outputs are important to the organization. The employees also deserve to know what level of production is expected of them, and the precision with which they are to deliver their outputs.

This responsibility is closely related to the need to explain line of sight, but it's more than that. As explained in chapter 5, the line of sight concept means that the employees need to know how their work fits into the bigger picture of producing final outcomes for the organization. They need to see what part their outputs contribute to the development of final outcomes. They must understand why their output is important and must be produced in a certain way. Their output needs to provide the platform for the production of the next-level product. They must understand how to produce their products efficiently and in the proper format to facilitate efficiency at the next production level.

Understanding line of sight helps build expectations. But your staff need more to fulfill the need for clear expectations. They need to know if there are deadlines and what overall volume of output is expected from your unit each day and each week. They need to have that unit-level output translated into individual output levels and delivery times. They need to understand the consequences if they fail to deliver on time and in proper volume.

The employees also deserve to know how you will gauge their success. This means you must let them know what measures you will review to determine the unit's success, how you will analyze reductions in output, and what options are available to make corrections.

You should also find ways to publicize production trends in your unit. For example, you could maintain a production chart outside your office, showing weekly or monthly production volume, timeliness of delivery, and output per person. You could even trend the range of individual production levels (without showing names) so that staff members can see where they fit in. This type of visualization can show what's possible and provide incentives to become the highest producer.

If various members of your staff produce different outputs, you should explain the various roles in sufficient detail so that everyone has a general understanding of each function and how they are intended to fit together.

Your work group will certainly experience unexpected

complications from time to time. Something will happen in the chain that will affect your unit's production. During these times you need to keep your staff informed: let them know what has happened, how it is being addressed, and whether there is a resultant change in expectations from them. For example, if one of the inputs to your unit's work is experiencing delays, your staff will be unable to continue routine production of their outputs. Keep them apprised of the situation—what is being done to restore the input operation, how long the issue is expected to persist, and what alternative activities your unit will undertake in the interim. If the result of the issue is that your unit's production will diminish by 15 percent for the month, the staff should be informed.

The discussion above relates to your conveyance of clear expectations to your general work team. You also need to let staff members know their individual performance expectations and how they are performing in their key work areas. My experience is that this component of performance management is one that many managers dislike, and it is a component that is poorly executed.

You can't manage your team and your people without being attentive to performance management. As we have already discussed, setting up the right performance metrics is fundamental. Having regular, scheduled discussions with each individual on your team is also a basic need. Almost everyone wants to do a good job and be perceived as a positive contributor. Everyone is sensitive to the boss's perception of their performance. So don't hide from this management responsibility.

The more open your performance management procedures, the more likely they'll be accepted as a normal part of business. That doesn't mean you share the content of individual performance feedback with the whole team. Rather, it means you make the process open and public, so everyone knows what to expect. You will gain acceptance more quickly if you make the process public but honor the privacy of each individual's discussion and feedback.

As an example, suppose you have a work process where you have five staffers doing the same function who are producing the same outputs. You need to make it publicly clear that the unit needs to produce twenty-five units per week and maintain 95 percent accuracy. You publish the unit's results each week but do not share the individual's performance numbers with the group. You could post outputs for each anonymous individual's numbers—you say, for example, that employee #1 had twenty-five outputs at 95 percent, employee #2 had twenty-six outputs at 94 percent, and so on. By setting up your feedback process this way, you keep it objective and give your staff perspective on their performance.

As you conduct individual performance feedback sessions, it will become rapidly apparent why it's important to have performance metrics that reflect the core activities of your staff and collect data in an objective way. Performance feedback is very personal for the recipient. You need to tell each staff member how he or she is doing, and you need to provide some detail, so your discussions should relate directly to the individual's performance plans. If it states he or she should produce on average ten widgets per day, and his or her accuracy or precision level should be 95 percent or higher, you should have data on those performance elements and target your discussion directly toward the person. If employee #5 produces thirteen widgets per day, you need to let that individual know his or her production is consistently and significantly above expected levels.

Production metrics are relatively simple to discuss. The number of widgets produced and the precision levels can be objectively gauged. Conveying performance is straightforward. The areas of teamwork and interpersonal interactions can be more difficult. Objective data is not as readily available in these areas. But you must include these areas in your feedback, and keep the discussion focused and professional. It's not sufficient or acceptable to tell an employee, "You're hard to get along with." It *is* appropriate to remind an employee that you have had to intervene with his or her work group four times over the preceding four months to soothe egos and focus discussions and that each time, that particular employee was involved in the disagreements.

As stated above, it's important that you quantify an employee's performance when you offer feedback. If production is consistently above the expected level, praise is in order, sometimes followed by a reward. If production has slipped below the minimal acceptable level, you need to explore remedial actions. Closer supervision or training may be needed. You should give these concepts some thought before your feedback session, so you are prepared to discuss the issue(s) with your employee. Performance management is about assessing current output levels, rewarding high achievement, and designing ways to improve deficient areas. Gear the discussion toward improvement, not punishment.

When an employee develops problems in production or in behavior, your first reaction should be to devise an improvement plan. Only when a problem becomes persistent and unresponsive to improvement attempts do you want to look at disciplinary actions, but when a problem is clearly resistant to corrections, you must explore more serious options.

When people apply for jobs, the announcements routinely include education and experience expectations. So the applicants who later become the selectees should know these expectations. It is your responsibility to let your people know the expectations for continuing education and development of additional competencies. You should also provide assistance—or solicit assistance from your personnel department—to offer training opportunities in areas of critical competencies so staff can see opportunities to strengthen existing skills and develop new ones, increasing their value to the organization.

Hopefully, your organization provides a dynamic environment so that opportunities for promotion and growth are available. As part of your ongoing supervision, you should let your staff know what you see as their strengths and which areas could use further development.

You need to distribute training and developmental opportunities fairly among your staff.

Developmental assignments can be valuable in promoting staff growth. If your organization does not have a systematic way for offering developmental assignments, you have an opportunity to help the organization by starting such a process. You can work with sister staff managers to create developmental assignments that allow people to learn the elements of other jobs, see the organization from new perspectives, and build new skills. Such efforts will pay for themselves many times over and will encourage your staff to be creative and look for growth opportunities.

You want them to grow and move on. You want to have mechanisms in place so you can welcome new generations of employees, build their skills, and move them on as well. You want your staff to recognize a place where people are nurtured and developed and know your people have a strong record for promotions. When this is the case, you will not have any difficulties recruiting open positions.

In addition to training and developmental assignments, you can use quality control results as skill development opportunities. All right, some of you are laughing as you read that last sentence. *Nobody* uses quality control results for skill development, you say. You may be right. But quality control results should be a valuable training tool.

Your quality control reviews should assess processing correctness at midprocess or at incremental steps in the overall process. These reviews should provide insight into each step of the operation. If any step is completed improperly, it may affect production at later steps and increase the possibility of an insufficient or inaccurate result. We all make mistakes, so the quality control review will surely find some errors. The assessor needs to ascertain whether an error is simply a loss of concentration, an anomaly, or if it potentially represents a recurring operator error. By doing several reviews on each operator and then reviewing appropriate data, the assessor can determine whether an error reflects poor operator understanding of the process. In those circumstances some level of training may be appropriate. You need to have a follow-up mechanism in place to advise employees of recurring process errors and give them guidance on the proper approach.

The value of this quality control operation is twofold. First, processing deficiencies will be identified quickly, before they have significant bearing on overall outputs. Second, you will identify areas of operator weakness and possible deficiencies in procedural instructions, so your staff will gain efficiencies.

Chapter Tips

- Develop a relationship of trust with your staff. This will facilitate positive communications and lead to effective results.
- You are the conduit of information from your boss to your staff. Keep the staff fully informed about the boss's priorities and concerns, including the good, the bad, and the ugly about your operation.
- Give your staff clear expectations about outputs, priorities, and deadlines.
- Let staff know how they will be evaluated, and incorporate regular performance reviews.
- Don't ignore the need to develop staffs' skills and competencies.

CHAPTER 10
PARTNERING THROUGHOUT THE ORGANIZATION

You need to establish and maintain good, positive relationships with other staffs. There are other staffs that feed work to your team and those that rely on your team to feed them work. There may be other staffs that share resources with you to accomplish similar tasks. (These are your sister staffs.)

In all of these instances, you need to have an awareness of the intersections and seams between the various staffs. This chapter discusses basic approaches to maintain productive relationships with sister staffs.

You should have learned about these intersecting staffs when you conducted your initial environmental scan upon taking your position. Hopefully your review confirmed that the intersections and overlaps between your work groups supported the corporate strategy. Use that information to establish bonds with these sister staffs from the beginning. It is advantageous for each work group to understand that your work dependencies are by design and help increase effectiveness. So, hopefully you spent time early in your tenure learning where you share responsibility with other staffs and how your interactions could be optimized.

As with every other area of your work life, working effectively with other staffs and influencing them—managing sideways—requires good communications. These other staffs are truly your partners; you each influence the other group's ability to produce desired outcomes. You should make sure you have regular discussions with these partners to confirm that your joint efforts continue to support the corporate strategy in the most effective way. Sustaining a positive working relationship and having regular meetings is not optional; it's a necessary part of your support of corporate intentions.

How you arrange your discussions is not terribly important. You can schedule formal meetings between your staffs. You can have periodic one-on-one meetings with your colleagues—in your office, or over a cup of coffee. The important thing is that you have regular communications. Allowing too much time between discussions increases the chance that some complications will begin to grow between your staffs. This is unnecessary and easily correctable.

Working with other staffs requires cooperation and focus on improving outputs for both groups. Since neither partner will have supervisory authority over the other, influence will rely on the power of ideas. Your relationship with these intersecting staffs stems from your common work areas, so you should take time to frame your discussions and relationships around them. Everyone involved needs to understand that each staff is dependent on the other and that effective cooperation is in everyone's interest. With this in mind it is probably beneficial to take time with these intersecting staffs early in your tenure and go over the areas where work intersects. Each staff should present its understanding of where the staff's work overlaps, how each staff is performing in the common areas, and where there might be room for improvements.

Hopefully you will find that your sister staffs share your interest in pursuing this type of collaboration, and you will work toward consensus on issues. If there is doubt or hesitation when you initially broach the topic, spend the necessary time to explain your mutual dependencies and the mutually beneficial results that your collaboration can engender. Always remind yourself and your colleagues that your successful collaboration is not an optional nicety; it's necessary to achieve desired corporate outcomes.

As it is with your other work processes, line of sight is important at the "seams," or the boundaries of each staff's work, where you pass outputs to other staffs. In fact, it may be more difficult to sustain a line of sight when work product moves from one staff to another. This makes it important that you ensure the organizational architecture is effective and that you can demonstrate a clear line of sight from your staff's outputs, through your sister staff's outputs, to the ultimate organizational outcomes.

You need to work through these concepts with your sister staff so you share the same understanding of the processes, outputs, and outcomes. This will strengthen your work relationship and will enhance productivity.

These relationships with other staffs are important. Positive working relationships can make you more effective in your work. Conversely, friction or antagonism between staffs will almost certainly cause reduction in effectiveness of all involved. If friction is allowed to linger, both sides will become decreasingly likely to advise the other of emerging issues. The tendency to blame one another for new problems will grow, so set the right framework for your relationships. If you need to go out to lunch with your colleagues to build a more relaxed and trusting relationship, do it. If you need to dig into the details of your common work areas to demonstrate your commitment and solidify your interdependencies, do that.

Almost certainly, though, issues will arise between the staffs where you cannot reach consensus. There will be an impasse. In anticipation of this likelihood, you should devise a way to resolve such impasses early in your relationship.

Two methods of impasse resolution come quickly to mind. First, you can ask your mutual boss to resolve these issues. This has the benefit of providing an authoritative resolution. Neither of you will be able to deny the resolution. But this method also passes control to your boss and diminishes your own influence.

A second option would be to appoint a small team comprised of equal membership from each staff, and empower them to devise a solution. You would have to temporarily remove these team members from other duties while they dedicate themselves to impasse resolution. This team would be given a firm deadline. Appointment to these impasse resolution teams should be portrayed as a positive thing (and treated appropriately by management), and successful resolutions should result in reward and recognition for the team members. This approach would strengthen the bonds between your staffs and vest each of you more strongly in the relationship.

These two options are certainly not the only ones available. Find the approach that bests fits your relationship and keeps you at the table with your colleagues.

While you are building a positive collaboration with your sister staffs, you are also showing your boss that you can work and play well with others, as they used to say in grade school. This is important because your boss needs to be confident that you are addressing these inter-staff issues. He or she doesn't have the time and shouldn't need to be refereeing these relationships. If it comes to that, you will soon be on the carpet explaining all the corrective measures you *will* take to strengthen your work relationships.

Just as you periodically audit your internal functions, you will need to check your common work areas from time to time. You need to make certain that processes have not shifted in ways that could diminish effectiveness. You need to validate that any enhancements that have been put in place have had the desired effects. This type of review function should be done by teams that can represent the views of all involved work groups. The oversight and audits must be done objectively. If people begin to see any indications that the reviews are being biased to favor one staff over another, it could seriously damage all the hard work it took to build a productive relationship.

As a manager directing these functions, that's your job. You must make it perfectly clear that the inter-staff efforts are intended for mutual improvements, not to find ways to give one staff leverage over another. If this message fails to sink in, or if it fades, petty jealousies can begin to grow. People may feel resentful and that the efforts are not worth the costs.

You need to be gracious with your sister staffs. Be quick to give them credit publicly (e.g., with the boss) for your joint improvements and successes. Be very slow to point the finger of blame at your colleagues when problems arise.

This approach will pay big dividends for you. Your interest needs to be in producing the best results for the organization. Your effective cooperation with other staffs promotes that outcome. It is *not* in your best interest to promote your staff, or yourself, above the other teams. If you keep these concepts in proper perspective, and demonstrate that commitment through your actions, you will build trust and respect among the other teams. Take the right actions, for the right reasons. In the end, you will get the appropriate credit.

Chapter Tips

- Establish and maintain good, positive relationships with other staffs.
- Set up regular discussions with sister staffs; frame the discussions around common work areas and dependencies.
- Find simple, productive methods for resolving impasses.
- Collaboration with sister staffs will be appreciated by your boss.

CHAPTER 11
REFRESHING THE SYSTEM

In a relatively short time—a few months—you can take numerous steps toward effective management of your operation and your team. You can and should ensure proper alignment with the corporate strategy. You will have conducted initial reviews of various components of your operation and made some adjustments to improve efficiencies. You have built (or reaffirmed) a positive relationship with your colleagues on other staffs. You have made sure that you have appropriate performance measures in place along with an oversight process to keep everyone moving in the right direction. You have solidified a reward and recognition program to acknowledge successes.

So you should be able to coast from here on out, right?

Not a chance!

All the areas you addressed upon arrival will need periodic review and updating. It's up to you to set up the necessary review schedules, an appropriate protocol for conducting the reviews, and assign responsibility for conduct of each review.

You are confident that you made improvements to the various operations with the enhancements you implemented during your first review. Hopefully that will prove to be true. Inevitably, some work components will perform well from the outset, and some will encounter struggles. Also, there is always the possibility that your most effective and productive work teams will encounter complications over time, and their production numbers will decline. So you review and refresh the system, hopefully catching problems before they become significant.

Establish a schedule to conduct your reviews. By doing so you ensure that all appropriate work areas will get reviewed. Responsibility for the timing and the substance of the reviews can be clearly assigned, and protocols can be published to facilitate consistency of approach.

Having a review schedule is a good thing, but it should not restrict you from doing ad hoc checks on various work elements. Being systematic is a positive attribute for managers; however, systematic thinking should not lead to regimented behavior. Your operations are going to be dynamic; you need to be dynamic to manage them. When you see things that appear to be amiss, or when your oversight reviews show problematic signs, you need to look into those areas. Get enough information so you can make a sound determination on whether problems are building. If they are, do a more thorough analysis and get to the heart of the problem(s). Make necessary changes to operations and eliminate the issue while it is forming.

The need for periodic review and refreshment of each work process highlights the importance of having documented the systems and procedures associated with each work process. The officially approved procedural guidance will serve as the guide for conducting refreshment reviews, or systematic analyses. The assigned analyst will have to confirm that current activities are consistent with procedural guidelines and that published procedures are effective.

If current operations do not conform to guidelines, the analyst should document how current activities vary from published guidelines. It is also appropriate that the analyst investigate why changes were made to the process and how those changes have affected performance. If the changes or variances have caused deterioration, recommendations to adhere to published procedures and policies should follow.

If the review finds operational changes that have actually improved processing, the analyst needs to consider recommending that they be institutionalized. Also, in this circumstance, it would be prudent to review any similar operations to see if the same enhancements can benefit the other operations.

You are not exempt from the need to refresh. You need to check yourself from time to time; make sure you are managing operations the way you pledged to, doing the things you promised. Are you devoting the amount of time you need for the budget? For training? Performance oversight?

Just as the effectiveness of each work component needs scrutiny, so do your activities. You need to candidly assess how you are spending your precious time and determine the effectiveness of your actions across the board. If you don't look, you won't know where you are most effective. You won't change or improve.

Managing effectively requires being constantly attentive in several areas—there are multiple balls to keep your eye on.

Over time you will develop stronger intuition about your operations. You will feel when areas begin to stress. Having said that, I suggest it will be prudent to approach your work logically and think about it from a systems point of view. By doing so you can make sure all areas receive appropriate attention. As your intuition grows, you can rely on it to enhance the checks and balances you put in place.

Make sure to arrange your operations logically, so they can effectively produce the expected outputs. Be aware of the more vulnerable aspects of your operation and pay closer attention to them. Assume that things will tend to evolve, even if you don't want them to. Periodically reexamine your operations and work processes according to assumed and historical risk, so they cannot evolve into substantially different processes (and results). This systematic approach requires rigorous review and oversight of your operations. It requires flexibility to react to each issue with a fresh attitude and not be bound by prior assessments.

Stay familiar with performance metrics. As a manager, you don't need to have the most detailed knowledge of your operation's performance metrics, but you do need to be aware of trends, and you probably need to get regular briefings from the staffers who are most intimately aware of the metrics. These exchanges will keep you informed and maximize the probability that you will note performance anomalies early, enabling you to take corrective actions before they become problems.

Managing effectively requires you to take care of your people. Make your staff know what's expected of them. Treat everyone professionally and with respect and compassion. Staff members should be given regular opportunities for training or developmental assignments. Help them grow and expand their skill sets, so they can increase their value to the organization. Encourage their interest in moving up. Doing otherwise is shortsighted and selfish. You will be best served if your staff develops and moves on. You can then recruit and develop new staff members.

Run your operation in such a manner that builds confidence, trust, and consistency among your staff. In successful organizations, people know their boss and the organization will look out for them.

You have a right to expect hard work from your staff. You do not have the right to take them—and their hard work—for granted. Recognize achievements; acknowledge unforeseen complications that might have affected production, and mitigate expectations; know your staff well enough so that you can recognize and accommodate special circumstances. This type of management behavior will strengthen your bond with employees and promote a stronger organization. Producing outputs effectively is important, but it's not so important that it prevents you from having a humane organization where people care for each other. I think it's fair to conclude that your organization will not succeed over the long term if the staff, the people, don't feel appreciated or respected and don't feel committed to the organization.

Managing effectively requires that you be a good steward of

your operating funds. Expenditures must be made thoughtfully, and constant effort should be made to keep costs down. You can delegate the day-to-day budgetary expenditures, but you must stay familiar with the overall budgetary picture, provide policy guidance on operating and spending priorities, and ensure that pace of expenditures does not outrun funding flow. Find your comfort level in managing the budget.

Managing effectively means being a good team player. Collaborate willingly and effectively with partners in the organization. Be attentive to your boss's needs. Be confident in your abilities and your results, but at the same time keep your ego firmly in check. If you start to let things be about you, your effectiveness will quickly diminish.

To remain successful as a manager, you will need to keep a positive attitude. As I have stated before, managing is dynamic because work operations are dynamic. You will never get things running perfectly. Even if you get your operations functioning smoothly and effectively, your operating world is not static, so situations will evolve. Problems will surface. Even in work areas where you have recently devoted substantial efforts to correcting operational issues, new complications will arise. You need the right approach to keep yourself motivated and to avoid frustration.

Look at each work week as a new challenge, an opportunity to identify the next work issue to wrestle with, dance with, and fix. Your goal will not be to fix it for all time. Rather, strive to keep all operational elements in control while making the whole work area better. You want to maximize uptime and minimize downtime. Output measures should be showing gradual (although sometimes a surge is a good thing) and steady improvements.

For me this is what makes operational management rewarding—even fun! You can expect that there is always another operational challenge right around the corner. It probably will show characteristics of issues you have previously addressed, but it will also have distinct components. You need to conduct a new analysis each time and acknowledge that the last assessment you did in this area will likely not apply. You need to remain open minded and objective in assessing issues and devising corrective measures. Embrace each new challenge.

Chapter Tips

- All the systems and processes you set up will need periodic reviews. Set up a review schedule.
- Your management world is dynamic; be flexible to react to new issues.
- Take care of your people; develop their skills so they can assume more responsibility.
- Maintain a positive attitude.

SUMMARY

I have tried to describe situations that managers encounter and the actions they will take to keep their organizations moving. I have placed emphasis on building a solid foundation that will facilitate success. It's a beginning rather than a comprehensive instruction. I see managers as active players in the organization, not aloof puppet masters pulling strings from above. I see managers living in a world with ebbs and flows, subject to constant changes. Hopefully, this type of environment is appealing to you. If it is, you will likely find an operational management position to be a good fit.

One thing you must remember is that as you manage your organization, other people may have differing views or criticize your actions. Don't be daunted by this; it's easy to criticize and not so easy to be responsible for results.

As Theodore Roosevelt said in his "Citizenship in a Republic" speech, delivered at the Sorbonne, Paris, on April 23, 1910:

> It is not the critic who counts; not the man who points out how the strong man stumbles, or where the doer of deeds could have done them better. The credit belongs to the man who is actually in the arena, whose face is marred by dust and sweat and blood; who strives valiantly; who errs, who comes short again and again, because there is no effort without error and shortcoming; but who does actually strive to do the deeds; who knows great enthusiasms, the

great devotions; who spends himself in a worthy cause; who at the best knows in the end the triumph of high achievement, and who at the worst, if he fails, at least fails while daring greatly, so that his place shall never be with those cold and timid souls who neither know victory nor defeat.

So let the critics say what they will. Rise to the challenge presented by the issues in front of you. Focus on what's best for your organization. Manage.

In a similar vein, management is about knowing and feeling your organization. You use that knowledge and intuition to analyze issues and devise corrective measures. Sometimes your proposed solutions will not work. Don't let that frustrate you. When a proposal doesn't have the desired effect, you need to analyze the reasons and use that information to develop a new proposal. Over time, if you learn from your missteps, you will become more effective, and a higher percentage of your proposals will succeed.

If you don't catalogue your experiences and learn from your missteps, you probably will not become more effective over time. As George Santayana said, "Those who cannot remember the past are condemned to repeat it" (1954).

Don't let setbacks frustrate you. Learn from them. As a manager you will face new challenges every day. You will never run out of opportunities to improve your effectiveness—your batting average, if you will. If you can keep an open mind and commit to continued learning, you will improve your management techniques, and your organization will gain from your value as a good manager.

APPENDIX A
COMPETENCIES

Communications—This is a broad and important area of competency. Managers need to constantly communicate with their bosses, peers, subordinates, and external stakeholders so that all parties understand requirements and expectations. Good managers understand the importance of what is communicated, to whom it's communicated, when the information is communicated, and the level of detail communicated to various recipients.

Compassion and Sensitivity—The understanding or empathy for the suffering of others. Awareness of the needs and emotions of others. In relationship to management, this relates to maintaining a human side to your business and keeping your hand on the pulse of the organization.

Creating Vision—This relates to giving your organization a clear view of where they are, where they are going, and how they are going to reach their destination.

Decisiveness—Exercising good judgment by making sound and well-informed decisions. Perceives the implications of decisions. Understands the importance of making decisions at the right time. When a situation is urgent, a strong manager will make a decision to move the situation forward, taking some risks if necessary, but weighing all available information to minimize that risk. Conversely, a good manager understands that if time is allowed, it might be most prudent to wait for receipt of all pertinent outlying information before making the decision.

Flexibility and Adaptability—Being aware of individual and business needs; being prepared to make internal and mechanical changes to better meet the needs of individuals and the business outcomes.

Honesty and Ethical Behavior—Characterized by fairness and straightforwardness.

Quick Study—Someone who can speedily learn the essentials of a task, especially a performer (such as an actor or a musician) with a gift for learning new material (such as lines, stage business, scores, etc.) at a remarkable speed.

Resourcefulness—Ability to deal skillfully and promptly with new situations, difficulties, and the like.

Self-Awareness— Awareness of one's own personality or individuality (m-w.com). For management purposes, self-awareness involves awareness of how your words and actions affect the organization.

Understanding and valuing diversity—Diversity means being composed of elements, qualities, or types of people. Managers need to understand the value of having and encouraging varying analytical approaches, worldviews, and academic preferences in their operations; also, diversity may add sophistication—and certain risks.

FUNDAMENTAL ACTIVITIES

Building and Sustaining Relationships—Anytime you have activities that involve more than one person, success will depend, at least in part, on how effectively each component works with other components. One element is often dependent on the outputs of another. Sometimes a component relies on the actions of an outside entity. The ability to identify, build, and sustain these critical relationships is fundamental to successful management.

Change Management—Change management refers to a systematic, reasoned approach to designing and implementing change in an organization.

Leading Employees—Leading includes the process of motivating others to work to meet specific objectives. Leading is also one of the key aspects of a manager's job. If the managers do not make any effort to help their employees to be successful in their job, and to take pride in their efforts, the employees are increasingly likely to start feeling lazy and they may not put any effort to the work they are completing.

Motivational Behavior—Keeping staff fully engaged in their roles and enthused about what they are doing. Good motivational behavior requires a lot of time and effort. It includes formal avenues for recognition of achievements, as well as informal notes of appreciation. It includes regular reminders to staff that their efforts are important to organizational success. It includes provision of avenues for personal growth, so that employees understand that growth opportunities may follow hard work and achievement.

Oversight and Accountability—This overlaps heavily with performance management and includes observing and analyzing the organizational performance at all levels, ensuring that all employees know how their work is observed and analyzed, and that regular, recurring feedback is expected and provided. That feedback is based on public accountability measures.

Participative Management—An open form of management where employees have a strong decision-making role. Participative management is developed by managers who actively seek a strong, cooperative relationship with their employees.

Performance Rewards and Recognition—This involves ensuring that appropriate performance systems are in place and tracking the right measures. It further involves regular use of the systems to gauge organizational and individual performances. Lastly, it includes the use of fair and public rewards and recognition for positive achievements.

Personnel Management and Development—The management of an organization's workforce, including responsibility for the attraction, selection, training, assessment, and rewarding of employees, while also overseeing organizational leadership and culture, and ensuring compliance with employment and labor laws.

BIBLIOGRAPHY

Belasco, James. 1990. *Teaching the Elephant to Dance*. New York: Penguin Group.

Bennis, Warren, and Burt Nanus. 1985. *Leaders—The Strategies for Taking Charge*. New York: Harper and Row.

———. 1985. *Leaders*. New York: Harper & Row.

Bennis, Warren. 1985. *On Becoming a Leader*. New York: Perseus Books.

Bolman, Lee G., and Terrence E. Deal. 1995. *Leading with Soul*. Hoboken, NJ: Jossey-Bass.

———. 2003. *Reframing Organizations*. Hoboken, NJ: Jossey-Bass.

Collins, Jim. 2001. *Good to Great*. New York: HarperCollins.

Drucker, Peter F. 1954. *The Practice of Management*. Harper and Row. New York.

Gladwell, Malcolm. 2013. *David and Goliath*. Little, Brown and Co. New York.

Goldratt, Eliyahu M. 1984. *The Goal*. North River Press. New York.

Hammer, Michael, and Steven A. Stanton. 1995. *The Reengineering Revolution*. HarperCollins. New York.

Krzyzewski, Mike. 2000. *Leading with the Heart*. Warner Business Books. New York.

Lawler III, Edward E. 1986. *High-Involvement Management*. Hoboken, NJ: Jossey-Bass. New York.

Liff, S. 2007. *Seeing Is Believing: How the New Art of Visual Management Can Boost Performance throughout Your Organization*. Amacom. New York.

May, Matthew E. 2007. *The Elegant Solution*. Free Press. New York.

Osborne, David, and Ted Gaebler. 1992. *Reinventing Government*. New York: Penguin Books.

O'Toole, James. 1995. *Leading Change*. Hoboken, NJ: Jossey-Bass.

Peters, Thomas J., and Robert H. Waterman Jr. 1982. *In Search of Excellence*. New York: Warner Books.

Roberts, Wess. 1985. *Leadership Secrets of Attila the Hun*. New York: Hachette Book Group.

Russell, Bill. 2001. *Russell Rules*. New American Library. Harmondsworth, Middlesex, England.

Santayana, George. 1954. *The Life of Reason, or, the Phases of Human Progress*. New York: Charles Scribner's Sons.

Senge, Peter M. 1990. *The Fifth Discipline*. New York: Doubleday.

Walton, Mary. 1986. *The Deming Management Method*. New York: Putnam.

Wooden, John, and Steve Jamison. 2007. *The Essential Wooden*. McGraw-Hill. New York.

Printed in the United States
By Bookmasters